HEALING THE
Father Wound

HEALING THE

Father Wound

KATHY RODRIGUEZ

Pleasant Word
A Division of WINEPRESS PUBLISHING

Pleasant Word (a division of WinePress Publishing, PO Box 428, Enumclaw, WA 98022) functions only as book publisher. As such, the ultimate design, content, editorial accuracy, and views expressed or implied in this work are those of the author.

This book includes stories in which the author has changed people's names and some details of their situations to protect their privacy.

Unless otherwise noted, all Scriptures are taken from the *Holy Bible, New International Version®, niv®*. Copyright © 1973, 1978, 1984 by the International Bible Society. Used by permission of Zondervan. All rights reserved.

Scripture references marked kjv are taken from the King James Version of the Bible.

Scripture references marked nasb are taken from the New American Standard Bible, © 1960, 1963, 1968, 1971, 1972, 1973, 1975, 1977 by The Lockman Foundation. Used by permission.

ISBN 13: 978-1-4141-1045-5
ISBN 10: 1-4141-1045-6
Library of Congress Catalog Card Number: 2007904511

Dedication

This manual is lovingly dedicated to my husband, Rocky, who by the power of the Holy Spirit, fathers our children, Tim and Abby, like the father he never had. May the sins of the fathers stop with their generation and the love of our ABBA Father bless them to the thousandth generation.

Contents

Preface

One morning in 1992, armed with seven years of counseling experience on inadequate fathering, I eagerly zoomed out of my driveway and headed to a day of continuing education. I hoped to get some answers about father-wounding at last. I thought I'd spend an easy day listening to Dr. Jane Myers Drew's insights on father-loss and go home with six to eight hours of continuing education credit under my belt, ready to give definitive answers to a wide variety of clients who suffered because of issues with their dads. Boy, did God have a surprise for me!

Eight hours later, a more experienced and healed therapist drove into my driveway. Those six hours of systematic, experiential exercises designed to identify my own father woundedness did more to cleanse me of the ghosts from my past than any seminary graduate course I'd taken to date. For years I had walked people through minefields of chaotic relationships and unmet needs stemming from poor relationships with their fathers. I'd cried out to God for better understanding of the effects of fathering, hoping to find a clearer path to the truth. Little did I know that God would bring His answers to my questions in the form of the effects of father-wounding to the benefits of father-loving.

Jesus best illustrated the intended relationship of children and daddies when He said, "Let the little children come to me." He portrayed a representation of His own father that is warm, open and welcoming. He referred to God in heaven as His Father and ours in John 15. He taught His disciples to pray, "Our Father who art in Heaven..." in Matthew 6:9-13. The apostle Paul urged us in Romans 8:15 and Galatians 4:6 to cry out to our ABBA Father in heaven. God in heaven has made it very plain that He wants and desires above all else to be a daddy to His children.

Today, as never before, our children and our nation need a strong father presence. But as Frank Ancona states so eloquently in his book *Crisis in America: Father Absence,* "Once upon a time, America was the greatest nation on the face of the earth. Once upon a time, there were fathers in America."[1]

What has happened to fathers in America? Their absence has left a legacy that will far outlast the positive breakthroughs the men's movement made in the 1990s. We are feeling the consequences of a fatherless generation. Even just a few of the fatherless statistics cited by Paul Lewis in *Five Key Habits of Smart Dads* can leave us staggering:

- Fatherless children are twice as likely to drop out of high school.
- Principals across the nation report aggressive, acting out behavior, especially from boys who come from single-parent homes.
- Fatherless daughters are ninety-two percent more likely to fail in their own marriages.
- Fatherless sons are 300 percent more likely to be incarcerated in state juvenile institutions.
- Seventy percent of all young men incarcerated in the U.S. come from fatherless homes.
- Children from fatherless homes are failing in school, not because of intellectual or physical impairment, but because they are emotionally incapacitated.[2]

We as a society reap the consequences of a fatherless generation whether we like it or not. The woundedness is there all around us and in us. If we are to prevent the effects of fatherlessness from

Preface

spilling to the next generation, healing in our nation must bind up the brokenhearted who suffer from father woundedness, and also provide men with powerful hands-on guidance in effective fathering. The men's movement of the 1990s, as well as powerful men's Christian organizations such as Promise Keepers, have done much to educate men and fathers. However, we have generations of wounded men and women who are blinded by their own father wounds. Often, they do not know how to give what they have not received.

Secular books and research address and identify the effects of fatherlessness and inadequate fathering. Some Christian authors have attempted to address our need for heavenly fathering and drawing closer to Him. However, few books have integrated timely clinical research on fatherlessness with the host of research on how children develop a concept of God in their lives. Scriptural references, principles, and insights are offered here to produce a comprehensive and systematic healing process for the father wounded who seek to grow up in Christ. In this book I provide a tried and true structural process for "throwing off what hinders us and the sin that so easily entangles, letting us run with perseverance the race that was marked for us" (Heb. 12:1). My desire is to address the woundedness of the fatherless and provide a systematic healing process to bring us all closer to our ABBA, Daddy, so that He can teach us to father ourselves and the next generation in His image and to His glory.

CHAPTER 1

Ghosts from the Past

It was a typical drive home from church that Sunday ten years ago. Little did I know that it would prove to be a keystone in my healing journey. The kids began to grumble in the back seat, because it was lunch time and there was no food on the horizon. Typically my husband, Rocky, and I would discuss the meal possibilities on the way home from church. This particular Sunday I remember I felt tired and unmotivated to throw together a three course meal once we got home. I tentatively suggested, "Why don't we go out for a late breakfast?"

Rocky glanced quickly at me and asked his "favorite" question, "How much money is in the checkbook?" Marshaling my defenses for the presumed battle looming ahead, I shot back, "It's always about money with you, isn't it? There's never any concern about me or a desire to make my Sunday a little easier. It's always about how much money we have any time I want to take a little time off."

Rocky, barely managing to keep the car from running off the side of road, defended himself angrily but shrewdly, "I am not your father! Don't confuse me with him. Money is an issue you have with him, not me!"

As I stewed in frustration and confusion, I had to admit he was right. Here I was again, fighting this old battle with my long-deceased dad. At that point, all I knew was that I had deep pain and emptiness when it came to my relationship with my dad. Later I realized I was transferring that old hurt and unfinished business from my childhood onto my relationship with my husband in order to try and bring closure to my pain. Perhaps in doing so I would gain a sense of control over my past so it would not haunt me anymore. In the process, Rocky was getting the blame and fallout for issues I had never worked out with my dad. If I wasn't careful, I could end up seeing my husband as the same uninvolved, uncaring person I thought my father was. To his credit, my husband will never take the rap for someone else's mistakes, and this Sunday was no exception. He had heard this dialog once too often for his taste, and knew that who I was plaintively crying out to for loving understanding was not really him, but my own distant daddy.

Maybe at some time in your life, you've worn the same shoes I wore that Sunday afternoon. Perhaps there have been times you could swear you were arguing with your father instead of your spouse. Or perhaps you have been hurt by the lack of attention from others who you perceive act just like your distant, uninvolved father. You think you're hearing or seeing your father's treatment of you in someone else's actions.

Father-wounding left unattended can make it difficult for us to achieve the intimacy God created us to seek; to be known fully and yet unconditionally loved, and to give that kind of love and acceptance to others. When we don't receive adequate fathering in the form of nurturing, acceptance, support, and approval we can feel something is missing from ourselves. As adults, we unconsciously search for someone or something to fill this empty space, often believing that our happiness depends on finding just the right person to complete us. While secular and Christian psychologists agree that no other human being can complete us, many of us still search for an "illusive" phantom piece or person to complete us and make us feel good about ourselves instead of feeling inadequate. Where Christians and secular scholars disagree is whether God, as our heavenly Father, can be that provision for which we so desperately search.

Many of us yearn to be loved and accepted unconditionally, but do not feel worthy of it because our fathers never affirmed our value. In our desperation, we can settle for temporal substitutes in the form of people, chemical substances, work, ministry, etc., as long as it stays with us and makes us feel good about ourselves. The pain of a father-wounded person often takes on a life of its own, causing us to repetitiously reenact addictive patterns we've learned through the years to get these father-needs met. This can leave our adult lives so preoccupied with getting our own long-unmet needs fulfilled that we have nothing to give anyone else. By not having fully bonded with the first and most important male in our lives, we often gravitate to individuals who help us recreate this sense of emotional deprivation, which resets the stage to reenact our addictions again. It exhausts us!

Men especially can be hurt from inadequate fathering and set up for addictive behaviors. Men of previous generations were often socialized, through male role models in their families, not to display emotional needs. Many learned to stuff these needs and feelings away, pretending they did not exist so as not to risk not fitting in with other males. Tragically, men whose needs have not been met adequately by dad often have not learned how to interact with women in an equitable fashion. They often model unemotional, male behavior they learned from their fathers. If his dad modeled a distant and emotionally unavailable relationship with his mother, little Johnny may very well see this as the way men act like men. Still others may be sophisticated enough to figure out honey draws more flies than vinegar, and through a mother's example of nurturing may be able to provide some degree of love and support to a spouse. However, without the male role model of dad sustaining a loving and affection-ate relationship with his mother, big Johnny can feel at a loss to know how to go the distance in a loving and intimate relationship.

Women without adequate fathering can grow up searching, but making unrealistic demands for support, protection, and love from loved ones. They often cycle between idealizing their husbands and feeling disappointed when they perceive their husbands don't meet their needs. The reason? She has no male standard with which to measure her partner's love and affection. She has no idea how much or how little she needs. She's working without a blueprint, if you will. She doubts whether she is truly lovable, because she's never experienced it. And her unrealistic demands for love and affection often push away any chance for her to receive love as an adult.

Psychologists call this process of working out past conflicts with people in our present, "transference." Whenever we transfer an unresolved conflict from the past into a relationship in the present, we unconsciously attempt to work out that old conflict.[1] There's just one problem. We're most often trying to work it out with the wrong person! The conflict lies with a person in our past, not the person standing before us in our present. Meier, Minirth, and Wichern state that, "Children who are deprived of a loving relationship in the home grow up feeling undeserving or inferior. They attempt to prove that they are somebody by emphasizing their appearance, their accomplishments, or the status value derived from social position. Because a self-image based on those areas is always conditional on their continuance, a false security factor develops. People get caught up in self-verification or in constantly proving to themselves that they are NOT a nobody."[2]

If my counseling load is any testimony, I don't think I'm alone in trying to work out yesterday's conflicts with my dad with my husband or other significant males in my life today. My experience in listening to many of my clients' stories over the years reveals one thing very clearly—there is no substitute for good fathering. Fathers are the most pivotal person in their children's lives. If dads don't love and attach to their children properly, they set in motion a legacy of pain that can extend for generations. God created human beings to attach to one another and develop strong affectionate bonds.[3] The earliest relationship in which a child's natural need to attach begins is the relationship with parents. Psychological research into the theory of attachment is quite robust in documenting the emotional distress when these early attachments with significant others are disrupted, especially in the early years of childhood. However, God's Word supersedes all research in successfully predicting the scars that children would bear due to the sins of their fathers when He says in Exodus 34:7, "the sins of the fathers will be passed on to the third and fourth generations." Therefore, it is no accident that our current society bears the effects of father-woundedness through conflicts with mates, significant others, best friends, bosses, and social relationships in general.

If you still battle invisible childhood hurts inflicted at the hands of someone who was supposed to love and protect you from everything evil in the world, there is hope available. Are you still trying to get that one special person to know you are alive? Do you struggle with acceptance and proving yourself to significant others? Are you still trying to love and accept yourself after all these years? Do you struggle with authority figures? If you answered yes to any of these questions, you may have a father-wound. There is hope and healing available in the next few chapters. But first we have to uncover the woundedness so we can apply this healing process properly. Join me as we take a look at some varieties of father-wounding.

John is a 35-year-old man who hasn't yet decided what he wants to be when he grows up. Still on the small, wiry side, John was raised by a much larger father whose criticisms boomed over him every day and night of his existence. Nothing he said or did was ever good enough. His father called him a "loser" many times. Now as an adult, John has gone to graduate school off and on, but has a hard time following through on choosing a life direction or vocation. He drifts from one part-time job to another. He believes God has a calling on his life—he just can't decide what it is. He struggles with his own sexuality. By acting promiscuously, he temporarily experiences some vestige of love and affection that he missed from his dad. But these crumbs never last for long because they are not the genuine article. Maybe one day he will actually feel loved and accepted for who he is for longer than 20 minutes; however, his self-esteem and self-respect seem to be a filling tub with the plug missing. There is just never enough attention, affection, or sex to quite fill him up.

Or consider Elise, a 41-year-old single woman who has had many relationships in her life. She's searched high and low for Mr. Right. But whether she's searching in church or in a bar, Mr. Right never hangs around for long after he's quenched his thirst or added another notch to his belt. While Elise can attach and depend on a man quite easily, she has a knack for picking men who can't or won't attach themselves more permanently to her. Love appears elusive to her, yet it is the thing to which she is addicted. She fears she will never have the family she yearns for or that one true love she's been seeking most of her life. She believes that if she could just get the right guy's attention long enough, she could make him—and herself—happy.

Or maybe your story is more like Janet's. Janet never got to know her father because her parents separated and divorced before she was two years old. She had a stepfather, but he didn't seem too interested in making Janet feel like a daughter. In fact, he didn't seem too interested in Janet at all. Her birth father disappeared for years at a time, only to make sudden appearances after years of absence. Janet used to fantasize that her birth father would come back into her life one day as a reformed dad—having realized how much he had missed out on—and make everything better again. When she dreamed about him, Janet's birth father was always the most handsome, loving, and funny dad one could hope for. One day, Janet's birth father did come back. This time he stayed around for awhile. After he took her car and most of her cash with her ATM card, Janet discovered her dad was "mortal" after all.

Jordan's father physically abused him. Because of this, Jordan has never allowed anyone to get close to him, and never married. He's too afraid of having children that he might abuse just like his dad did. So Jordan is a loner. Although he has a God-given need to attach, he's too afraid to do it with real live people for fear he'll be rejected or found defective in some way. He still comes to church and sits in the back, but he's really too afraid and ashamed to have anyone get to know him. He buries himself in his work and his computer. His computer houses all Jordan thinks he can handle about relationships with people. The pornographic pictures on his screen occupy his solitary hours because they're as close as he wants to get to real people who could hurt him, or that he might hurt.

These are composite stories that represent numerous individuals I have counseled over the years who have one thing in common in the midst of all their separate circumstances and stories: they are father wounded. The quality of their lives and relationships have been shaped and driven, not by the power of God on their lives, but by the unconscious, haunting, missing vital connection they long for with their earthly fathers.

Maybe you can identify it in your own personal heart, that pressing need to be validated and loved by an authority figure in your life, or the satisfaction that comes when you know you're responsible for that twinkle in someone's eye. It really makes no difference whether you're a man or a woman. Little boys as well as little girls often don't have daddies who know how to love them and bring them up to face the world confidently. Some daddies are gone completely from their homes by way of death or divorce. Some fathers live physically at home, but are not mentally or emotionally available to their children. Other fathers verbally abuse and criticize their children to the point that their sons or daughters wish they weren't there. There are also fathers who have physically or sexually abused their children. All of these fathers are examples of inadequate fathering and can intentionally or unintentionally inflict invisible father wounds that fester and smolder into adulthood if left unattended and unhealed.

Before we look at these earthly fathers in greater detail, let's consider a different kind of father-resource for healing: our heavenly Father. David captures God's idea of father-love in Psalm 103:3-11 when he tells us that God promises to overlook our mistakes, to heal us from sickness, to redeem us, and to show us lovingkindness and compassion. God says He will satisfy our yearnings so we will feel renewed enough to soar like eagles. He further promises to be compassionate and gracious, slow to get angry and yet willing to set boundaries with us. He will never give us what our sins deserve, but will surround us with His compassionate grace as long as we honor Him. He knows us through and through, but accepts us anyway with His huge capacity for lovingkindness. How many of us can boast of an earthly father like this? Yet how many of us still yearn for a father like God promises to be?

If we take even a superficial look at the "fathers" of the Bible, we see that most of them also had feet of clay. Consider Adam, the first man, for instance. In Genesis 3, he blamed his mistakes on his wife, Eve, and ultimately God Himself, since He gave Eve to him for his wife. We read later that one of his sons killed the other. What about Abraham, known as the Father of Many Nations? Genesis 20 tells us he lied and pretended his wife was his sister to keep from being killed by a foreign king. Previously he had slept with his wife's maid because he had some doubts as to whether God could really make him the Father of Many Nations (Gen. 15–16). Later, in Genesis 22, after God produced the promised heir, Abraham tried to redeem his faith in God by almost slaying the son of the promise, Isaac, as an offering to the Lord because he knew God would rescue him. Although God told Abraham to offer Isaac up as an offering in the first place as a test of his faith, Abraham's "sacrifice" could be labeled "abusive" by today's standards. Or what about David, you may ask. David committed adultery, conspired to kill his paramour's husband, and counted his armies (2 Sam. 11-18, 24). Though God called him a man after His own heart, He also knew him as a man with blood on his hands. With David so busy with these extracurricular activities, is it any wonder he had little time to invest in fathering his children with the attention they needed? Absalom, one of David's sons, went on to try to wrest the kingdom from his father and fornicated with his father's concubines on the roof before the whole city! How's that for a testimony to your fathering?

One of the gracious displays of God's character is that He never gives us "perfect" role models in Scripture. Every Bible character or hero has at least one flaw and is in need of a Savior, just like you and me. Just like David did in Psalm 35 after being confronted by Nathan, many men and fathers recognize and repent from their sins and shortcomings. Some go on to rectify some of the wounding they have inflicted on their children, but many die before they can address these mistakes. Worse yet, many children continue to carry these wounds because their fathers are too proud and blind to repent.

Jesus says, "I have come to give you life and give you life to the fullest" (John 10:10). It is not His desire that we should continue to live in pain at the hands of someone who is not taking responsibility. At the point we realize that our earthly father's inadequacies overshadow the blessings our heavenly Father is trying to give us, we must make a choice. We must choose to analyze and increase our understanding of our own woundedness so we may put it out of our way, and get on with the mission God has for us within His great kingdom. Too often, we try to get on with the mission without taking sufficient stock of what may hinder us in the long haul.

Our enemy, Satan, counts on our lack of foresight and planning. He can and will lay snare after snare, pitfall after pitfall of our own pasts to trip us up and delay us in receiving the fullness of life Jesus has promised to His kids. That's why it is imperative that we know our woundedness and practice honesty with ourselves and God about who we are and where we've come from. I call this process "The Name It and Claim It Game."

We can use this process of honesty to enlighten us to pitfalls that may await us at any turn, or we can use it to wallow in so we don't have to grow beyond our problems. Excessive preoccupation and blaming keep us stuck in the mire of immaturity and fear. The paradox of healing is that you can never be free of the emotional bondage you bear without facing the realities of its effects in you. When we face these realities, they become known and can have no future hold on us. As Dr. Jane Myers Drew says, "Denial is not a river in Egypt."[4] Denial exists in our own minds. The enemy will use it to thwart the plans of the Almighty One if we cooperate with him and pretend we don't bear scars that others know we do. We're much better off to accept responsibility for our woundedness, as well as our giftedness. It can take years off the healing process!

GOD THROUGH A LOOKING GLASS

Social scientists have been intrigued for years by the possible effects of parental images on a child's concept of God. Studies have found that how a child views his parents correlates positively with how he views God. In particular, research has shown that children's images of their fathers, more than images of their mothers, correlate with their image of God. Finally, negative images associated with parents correlated with the most negative images of God.[5] Because human beings have a God-given need to attach to each other in relationships, God can often become the "perfect" substitute parent as children grow to adulthood and individuate from their earthly parents.[6] Therefore, we can see that our relationship with our parents, and in particular the father relationship, strongly determines how we view God.

In the next chapters, we analyze the effects of our father wounds on our relationships with others and view of God. Scripture says, "the truth will set you free" (John 8:32), but most of us know the experiential reality that "the truth can set you free, but first it will make you miserable!"

We can never truly grasp how wide and how deep is the Father's love for us if we do not look squarely at our need for Him. Let's walk together through the rock garden of your past, turning over a few of your rocks here and there to inspect the wounds of your heart. Together, we will play "Name It and Claim It" in order to identify and own the effects of these wounds. After we have grieved and memorialized our wounds, we will put them away forever and not return to them. We'll be ready for a great adventure—discovering and savoring the special gifting your loving Father God has placed within you and desires to fan into flame, if you will draw near to His Father-love.

CHAPTER ONE

Homework Questions

1. Consider your adult life. Do you have any compulsive behaviors that cause trouble for you or someone close to you? Are any of these wounds specifically tied to your relationship or lack of relationship with Dad?

2. Do you ever find yourself in an argument with your spouse, your child, or some other close friend or relative that is really not about what's happening in the present, but is really tied to an unresolved hurt in the past? Do you see any patterns of "transference" in your relationships?

3. How far has your "search" taken you to fill the emptiness of your soul? Do you have a history of broken, abusive, or inadequate relationships? List them.

4. Pray and ask God to illuminate the areas of hurt in your life that are tied to your earthly father.

5. Observe relationships between fathers and their children this week, or remember a time when your dad seemed close to you. Draw this memory or present day observation with your non-dominant hand. (If you are right handed, this would be with your left hand and vice-versa. Non-dominant hand drawings often reveal more of a child's perspective than those of our more sophisticated dominant hand.)

MEMORY GRAPH

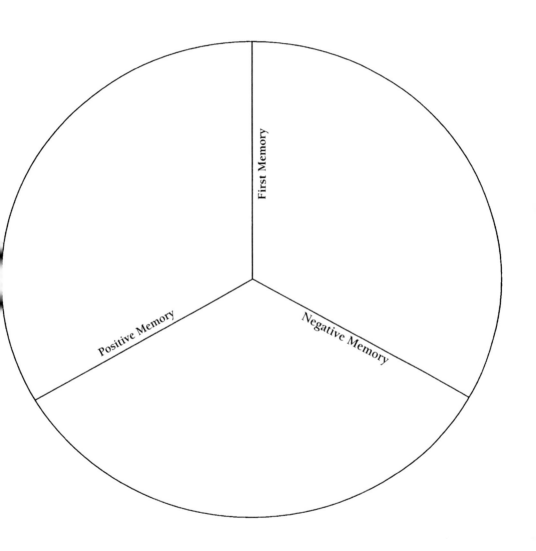

The Missing-In-Action Dad

eals of childish laughter pierced my solitude as I looked out the window at yet another drizzly day of Oregon rain. "Well, at least the weather isn't spoiling their fun," I thought, as I smiled to myself and considered how lucky my daughter was to have a daddy who could make her giggle so hard. My husband was threatening her again with "40 kisses" if she didn't stop whatever childish prank she was pulling on him. I ascended the stairs to gaze thoughtfully at the scene they created as they tumbled one more time across our Queen-sized bed. My daughter squealed at the top of her lungs as her daddy made yet another lunge for her, but I caught the gleam in her eye. She knew she had him now! Just as she intended from the beginning of the game, she had secured his undivided attention and set a twinkle in his eye. And she enjoyed it to the hilt. When Rocky came up for air, I saw that his eyes danced. "I don't know who caught whom," I thought. They both seemed quite sure they were responsible for the other's "twinkle" and were the supreme object of each other's affection.

"How interesting," I mused to myself, "that Rocky could give affection so unselfishly to our daughter when he never received any from his own father."

"He can give because I give through him," the Holy Spirit gently reminded me. I smiled a bittersweet smile to myself as I pondered the Holy Spirit's soft reminder.

Rocky grew up in a single-parent family. His dad chose not to be a father and husband to his family, but chose to father and live with a second family just two doors down the street without divorcing his first family. Rocky grew up in the shadow of that second family, attending school and playing with his half brothers and sisters in the street between the two houses. He witnessed his father giving them what he refused to give Rocky's family—attachment and support. Rocky's dad was what many of my father-wounded group members refer to as "The Missing-In-Action"dad.

This type of inadequate fathering is characterized by dads who prematurely leave the family scene, through divorce, death, suicide, military service, or who work away from their homes for significant periods. These situations often spell desertion and abandonment to the children left behind. Whether or not their father intended the desertion, children with this abandonment legacy are often left with two undesirable choices to defend against the gaping hole of natural longing for a male father figure to protect and guide them through life. The first choice is to begin the lifelong, unconscious search to find something or someone to fill this gaping hole of need in their life, which can lead to chemical substitutes or people substitutes, such as serial relationships.

The second alternative is to go through life replicating their father's example of emotional detachment, thereby robbing their own children of a feeling parent. This pattern numbs them to others' feelings and responses that might touch their own woundedness. A lack of emotional expressiveness perpetuates itself into subsequent generations, and father-woundedness becomes transgenerational. Either of these alternatives produces deep psychological roadblocks to emotional maturity.

Children who belong to single-parent families often grow up in double jeopardy. Not only do they know the fear of abandonment and a sense of incompleteness on an intimate basis, they often feel stigmatized as well. "Why don't I have a daddy?" they often ask. Or worse yet, they may worry that something is wrong with them because they do not have fathers like many of their friends. They often feel "different" or "ashamed."

The father who intentionally or unintentionally chooses to leave his children before or after they're born can leave behind a legacy of confusion and pain for his children to sort through. Because children do not develop enough cognitive complexity to be able to see any other point of view than their own before the age of five or six, they are often left with the perception that somehow they are responsible for their father's departure.

Jean Piaget, a noted Swiss psychologist, was one of the first to theorize about how a child thinks after observing his own daughter's thinking process. Prior to the age of seven, young children can think only in a concrete or literal fashion. While adults may be able to step back mentally from a situation and entertain multiple explanations for it, children do not.[2] Instead children accept situations at face value and do not do a lot of introspective investigation of the whys and wherefores. If Dad leaves them, the situation is about them and Dad, not about the divorce between Dad and Mom or the war that dad had to go fight, etc. According to Piaget, children do not even begin to develop abstract thinking until early adolescence. Therefore, to the young child, there are no other possible reasons for Dad to leave except for them. As kids see it, they are the center of the universe. Piaget terms this center-of-the-world thinking as egocentrism. Therefore, Dad's leaving is about them or caused by them.[3] "If I had been a better boy or if I had been quieter, then Daddy would have stayed," are reasonable thoughts to young children whose fathers leave them. "If my daddy can leave me even though he loves me, other people will leave me too," often becomes the invisible implication for a child's loss of father love.

Even if they are cognitively mature enough to understand their father may have had no choice about leaving, as in the case of death, their father's absence can create an emotional deprivation that will affect their lives for years to come. God has created us with a need to attach and belong. His word tells us as early as Genesis 2:18 that we were meant to be attached and in relationship with one another. "The Lord God said, 'It is not good for man to be alone. I will make a helper suitable for him.'" As Cloud and Townsend put it in their Christian bestseller *Boundaries,* "attachment is the foundation of the soul's existence."[4] When their earliest attempts to meet their created need for attachment and bonding are left unmet or interrupted, children are left unsecured or unanchored. They can drift through the ocean of life attempting to anchor, but not quite knowing how to attach or "tie up" properly to a secured port of significant relationship. This can wreak havoc in their ability to form satisfying relationships that can meet their soul's need for belonging. Due to the interruption in attachment, they don't know how to bond to the very thing they need the most, an attached relationship.

KATE

Kate finally realized that her father's suicide affected her ability to securely attach in her adult relationships. Her parents were happy in the beginning of their marriage. And they were ecstatic when Kate's mother became pregnant with her. After her arrival, Kate's father treated her like his little princess, carrying her everywhere. Even after Kate's little brother, Ron, came along, Kate was still the apple of her father's eye. She knew it and enjoyed the twinkle she could put there. Kate didn't know or understand then that those happy, playful times with her dad were infrequent oases to his tormented soul. The year before Kate was born, her dad served a year in Vietnam. Though he left the military when his tour was completed, those chilling memories of seeing his buddies die in foxholes around him never left him for very long.

Kate's arrival was a welcome distraction, but in the long hours of the night after she had gone to bed, her dad would try to anesthetize himself to his pain by drinking himself to sleep. Gradually, it took more and more alcohol each night to put him out of his misery. Then one morning he didn't wake her up as he usually did. At five years old, Kate lost her dad to alcohol poisoning.

Though his death was ruled an accidental suicide, Kate lost the object of her affection, her daddy. She felt abandoned and all alone. Her protector was gone! Her mother and grandparents, in shock themselves, thought it best that Kate not attend the funeral so she could remember her father the way he was with her the last time.

Like many others, Kate's family did not know how to deal with grief in an open fashion. Everything was hush-hush and cloaked in secrecy and whispers. If they did discuss it, they certainly didn't do it in front of the children. Through this whole process, Kate learned to be afraid that anyone she loved might abandon her. And because no one talked with her about her father's death, she grew up believing in a "little girl's perspective" of death even into adulthood. Though she remembered and treasured all the happy times with her precious daddy, she often felt deprived of that very same father affection and love and she searched for substitutes.

As a teen-ager she was vulnerable to boys who paid her the slightest bit of attention. If a boy smiled at her, she imagined that he wanted to be her boyfriend, and returned his friendliness ten times over. Unfortunately, the stars in her eyes turned to tears repeatedly over the years as boy after boy, then man after man, found her clingy, possessive, and insecure behavior too much to handle. Though the years wore on, Kate still dreamed that her knight in shining armor was right around the corner. It was as if a part of her was missing and she believed she would only be complete if she found this part of her in another human being: one who would finally replace the love and protection she had lost.

Kate's story is typical of women who've lost a father figure. They search and search. But try as they might, they just cannot find "daddy." Many even spend a lifetime searching for that "fantasy dad." It's as if they approach man after man asking, "Will you be my daddy?"

Still another take on the effect of the missing-in-action dad has to do with absent fathers who do come back into their children's lives later in adulthood.

CHARLENE

Charlene was pleased when she ran into her dad in a downtown department store during the Christmas holidays. She hadn't seen him in five years, but he still looked the same as far as she was concerned. She gave him her new telephone number, and he promised to call her to get together during the holidays. Charlene fantasized that now that she was an adult, perhaps her father would relate to her better and want to make up for time lost. "The key to keeping him around," she thought, "is not to bring up the past so he won't feel guilty and avoid me. Therefore, I'll make no demands of him and I'll be open to whatever he proposes."

After three weeks without a telephone call, Charlene finally called her dad herself. He said he was sorry he hadn't called, but he'd lost her telephone number. "Yes," he said, "I'd love to spend Christmas Eve with you and your family."

Though Charlene gave him detailed directions, Christmas Eve came and went without as much as a phone call of regret from her dad. During her counseling session the next week, she expressed her disappointment this way: "I thought sure he would follow through this time. I made it so easy for him. All he had to do was show up and show me he wanted to try to have a relationship with me. Is that too much to ask?"

Sadly, I had to tell Charlene, as I've had to break the news to numerous others over the years: "Yes, for your dad it may have been too much to ask."

Though divorce drives some men away from the relationship with their children, for others it can provide a setting of convenience; a way to avoid being close. If a father carries interrupted attachment experiences from his own family, he can drift. He may not know how to properly attach to his potential partners (hence, more interrupted attachments like divorce) or even his own children. Over the years, it can become a way of life not to get close to others because trying to attach himself to them is like an unsolved mystery. Therefore, it becomes easier and more convenient to actually avoid getting close because it represents an unknown and feels uncomfortable. If his parents did not nurture him, it is unlikely that he will be able to give away emotional support and nurturing that he never received or saw offered. Being close with others, exchanging love and intimacy breeds interdependence. That can be very frightening for adults who have experienced interrupted dependence upon their own parents' love and emotional support. This experience teaches them that it is not emotionally safe to trust and get involved with people who claim to love you.

Tragically we can see that one of the main ingredients feeding father-loss is chronic, unresolved, and transgenerational father loss. This is as true for men who grew up with a traditional father in the home as it is for men who grow up in homes where their fathers were not physically there.[5] Here we see the effects of God's promise in Exodus 34:7 in the "sins of the fathers" being visited on subsequent generations. Therefore, we can see the natural consequences to how men grieve the loss of their own fathers becoming central to perpetuating the legacy of father-wounding to the next generation.

JERRY

Jerry came to therapy because his girlfriend complained that he wasn't committed enough to the relationship. Though they had been together for three years, 37-year-old Jerry felt no closer to getting married than he had five years before when his last serious relationship ended. While he liked having someone around on a permanent basis, Jerry rationalized that he wanted someone to be there because they wanted to be with him rather than because they were married to him and had to stay. While Jerry's rationalization sounded very sophisticated, it covered over the real problem: Jerry suffered from father-hunger and had no idea how to commit and follow through with a relationship, because he had never witnessed it. Jerry's natural father left before he was born and his mother brought in a series of stepfathers over the years. Some of them were interested in Jerry and others not. What Jerry knew of relationships stemmed from what he had witnessed growing up. His mother would meet a man, they would hit it off, and soon he would move in with them. Then in six months, a year, at the most two years, that man would move on. The closest thing to a stable relationship Jerry had was with his mom, who always took care of him through all the live-in relationships.

Jerry liked his girlfriend, Heather, and maybe he even loved her. When I asked him how committed he was to the relationship, he could only shrug his shoulders and say, "I don't know." Heather was just the latest in a line of incomplete relationships for Jerry. He was good at "playing house," but words such as *commitment* or *permanency* were just not part of a comprehensible vocabulary for him. He moved in and out of one relationship after another. When the bickering and fighting outweighed the good times, Jerry knew it was time to move on. Sadly, Jerry seemed doomed to repeat the same mistakes, because of his inexperience with male role models who could adequately follow through and complete the attaching process. He was paying the price of previous generations of fathering in his family.

CAUTION: HEALING IN PROGRESS

I want to stop and sound a cautionary note here. While it is necessary to understand the "missing in action" dad's context and the possible early explanations for his ineffective fathering, his early childhood deprivation doesn't automatically cancel out or negate his children's perception of their own personal suffering at his hand. Oftentimes, I have had to caution father-wounded individuals from overly sympathizing with their father's pain and negating their own experience of pain by his hand. While it is true that a dad may have had inadequate preparation for fathering, once he had a child he became responsible before God to love and nurture that child the way Scripture says.

"Fathers, do not *exasperate* your children; instead, bring them up in the training and instruction of the Lord" (Eph. 6:4). What does Paul mean by "do not exasperate your children"? The New American Standard version refers to this part of the passage as "do not provoke your children to anger." And indeed a look at Webster's definition of exasperate verifies that it means "to make angry or irritated, to tax the patience of." Therefore, it would seem that fathers are enjoined by Paul to demonstrate awareness or concern for how their children perceive their behavior and to practice care and concern for their children's welfare. Colossians 3:21 in the NASB further amplifies Paul's admonition to fathers by stating, "Fathers, do not exasperate your children, that they may not lose heart."

Individuals who carry a father-wound by a "missing-in-action" dad are often so exasperated that they have lost heart. They've missed out on something they unconsciously know they should have gotten.

Therefore, let me say, "Pain is pain," whether it is a father's pain that results in his inability to attach and form loving, close relationships with his children, or whether it is the pain of the adult child who has lost heart at the hands of an exasperating father. Grieving father-loss requires an equal understanding of both perspectives.

Father-wounded individuals must learn to hold both experiences of pain, theirs and their father's, side by side in mutual tension. This may create cognitive dissonance or a disagreement in your head between two conflicting pieces of information. "Dissonance and consonance refer to the relationship that exists between two elements or thoughts."[6] Either these two thoughts agree with one another, i.e. consonance, or they appear to disagree with one another, i.e. dissonance. Your father's experience of the pain of his father-woundedness is neither more nor less valid than your experience of father-woundedness by him. You may feel internal cognitive pressure to invalidate your own pain, thinking your dad experienced more pain than you did. Or you may want to deny the reality of his pain to weigh in more heavily on your own. I suggest you try to equalize the pressure you may feel in looking at your experience and your dad's. Instead, allow this apparent dissonance to balance itself. Do not be afraid of a little internal pressure. After all, you've lived through the worst part, the experience of father-wounding itself. Prematurely resolving this pressure to be overly sympathetic to either your father's pain or your own won't solve the problem. Jesus knows both of you did without the emotional nurturing you needed. He went through both of your experiences with you. He felt the sting of emotional pain as each of you went without adequate love.

Remember—we do not serve a God who does not know our suffering. Hebrews 4:15-16 tells us that we have a high priest who sympathizes with us and encourages us to approach Him for support in our time of need.

Yes, your dad may have suffered father-wounding himself and did not know how to father you adequately. And he was the adult in your life and you were his child. As a parent, he took on the responsibility for your welfare and protection. If he didn't know how to love and nurture you due to his own brokenness, it was his responsibility to call on God to show him. Now that you have become aware of your own father-wounding, it becomes your responsibility to call on God to help you heal. Your healing is your responsibility to God. Leave your father's healing to him and his heavenly Father, ABBA-God.

Sadly, who among us has not made mistakes because we refused to bow our knee and humble ourselves and let God heal us from the inside out, making us into the new creations (and parents) He has promised to do in 2 Corinthians 5:17. To stem the tide of father-wounding to the next generation, we and our fathers need to repent from the mistakes and blunders we have made out of our own unhealed state of father-woundedness. However, we can only take responsibility for ourselves and leave our fathers to God. I'll discuss this more when we talk about forgiveness in an upcoming chapter.

Even if a father has a new family to distract him from his previous responsibilities to his firstborn children, he still carries the responsibility for all his children's welfare, not just those with whom he physically lives. Whatever the practical reason, unattached dads will often choose to make their absences permanent. This can and does provide the ultimate rejection and exasperation for his children.

The children of a dad who's missing-in-action can come to question the legitimacy of their own personhood and existence. From their perspective, the most important person in their eyes has looked at them and found them lacking. The implications for emotional well-being are piercing. What do they do now? How do they go on? The one person in the world that could validate their existence chose to walk away. Many are left feeling like a piece of themselves is missing, or worse, like somebody's discarded garbage.

However, there is one who does want us and can maximally validate us. Consider the words of Jeremiah: "The Lord appeared to us in the past saying, 'I have loved you with an everlasting love. I have drawn you with loving kindness" (Jer. 31:3). Or consider Marie Chapian's personalized devotional rendition of Jeremiah 31:3: "I call you with an everlasting love, constantly, constantly. If you were to think of yourself as I think of you, how different you would be."[7] The Lord God himself declares He loves you with an everlasting love. He attempts to "draw" or woo us to Him with loving kindness. We do not have to pursue this father longing for Him to love and protect us. He pursues us instead! What a concept to try to absorb!! Please allow yourself just a moment to take in this possibility.

FROGS AND PRINCES

As I have observed many women who carry father-wounds, I have been especially touched by the persistent and unrelenting hope individuals who've had missing-in-action dads possess. They never seem to lose hope that their father will one day find them and want them back. This fantasy is often characterized by an almost fairy godfather quality. There is the stubborn illusion that one day this bigger-than-life father will rescue them from their pain and magically make everything better with a wave of his wand. Father-wounded women often approach romantic relationships with the idea that the next man who comes along will be their all-knowing, all-sufficient prince. But alas, after several years of "togetherness," they often discover they have kissed yet another frog!

Research into parent-child relationships has shown that as children navigate themselves through becoming separate individuals from their parents, they can often create an "ultimate rescuer" figure who will shield the child from death or harm. While children usually fantasize this cosmic rescuer as a parent figure, adults often see this person as God. While this image is often idealized, it could be seen as an attempt to try to blend a child's perception of parent into a known perception of God rather than an unknown.[8]

Males who have lived through the experience of a missing-in-action dad have often been forced to grow up prematurely. They have not gotten to savor the innocence of a childhood without responsibilities. Some have even been "fathers" themselves to their brothers and sisters without having a clear idea or role model about being a dad. The boy without a father often has to buck up and deny his feelings of loss so he can set the example for the rest of the family, while providing "male protection" of which he has no clue.

Individuals who have fathers who are absent have no standard against which to compare every future man or authority figure. "Exactly what does the genuine article look like? Would I recognize a healthy father figure if I met one?" Anyone could be a protector, rescuer, mentor, or future mate. Individuals with abusive, critical, or emotionally detached fathers who physically live with them at least appear to have a flesh and blood standard of comparison, albeit inadequate. Missing-in-action dad sufferers don't have this same point of comparison. Therefore, they are more vulnerable to trying to form relationships with anyone, even individuals who aren't able to meet their needs. Future chapters will clarify the characteristics of safe and healthy authority figures and father substitutes. But first let's look at the real need and what will meet that need completely.

ABBA, THE MISSING LOVE OBJECT

It is my desire to show you, after we have uncovered all of your father-wounds, the great desire and capacity God has to be the father to the "fatherless." He is our true "missing love object." Attachment theorists have known for years that children look for someone who will love them as they are and will meet their needs. We will never feel complete without having ABBA in our lives and choosing to embrace ourselves with his all-sufficient, utterly incomprehensible supply of love and affection. He is the ultimate role model of a father. And He desires us not only to allow Him to father us but also to learn by His example.

As research has strongly suggested, a child's view of his parents is highly correlated to his developing representation of God. As children separate from more maternal-based needs, God can become the "perfect attachment substitute."[9] It is true that boys as well as girls connect nurturance to God, especially if Dad was nurturing and perceived as being similar to one's idea of God. Psalm 139:15-18 paints a picture of the ever-present nurturer David found in his ABBA-Father:

"My frame was not hidden from you when I was made in the secret place. When I was woven together in the depths of the earth, your eyes saw my unformed body. All the days ordained for me were written in your book before one of them came to be. How precious to me are your thoughts, O God! How vast is the sum of them! Were I to count them, they would outnumber the grains of sand. When I awake, I am still with you."

38

Just as David remembered, during times of stress and soul-searching, who he belonged to, we can also turn to our Father who is ever-present and desires our attachment to Him. He is the only thing that can fit into that gaping hole left by an inadequate earthly dad. Though we try to stuff in all kinds of substances such as drugs, food, jobs, or relationships, they just do not fill the hole completely so we won't ever feel needy again. There is only One who calls us to be that attached to Him, and it is in Him that we truly can find ourselves.

CHAPTER TWO

Group Study Questions

1. Do you have a Missing-In-Action dad?

2. What behaviors in your life may be connected to not being adequately attached to your dad?

3. What kind of attachment relationship do you wish you would have had with your dad?

4. Read and examine Ephesians 5:4 and Colossians 3:21. What does Paul mean by "exasperate," and what effect does it have on one's children?

5. How is your view of God affected or influenced by your father's behaviors?

6. What does Hebrews 4:15-16 say about Jesus' availability to us?

CHAPTER TWO

Homework Questions

1. Describe the circumstances of your father's absence. Was it due to death, military service, imprisonment, not being married to your mother, etc.? Do you remember when he left? Did he say goodbye? Elaborate any feelings or memories you have of his departure. Did you ever question why your dad left and wonder whether or not it was your fault?

2. How did your family process your dad's departure and absence? Was he ever discussed? Was your extended family open to questions or discussion about your losing your dad? Did your family offer any emotional support to help you understand your father's absence?

3. How does your dad's absence affect you now? Were you independent early, sort of like "a little adult?" Have you ever found yourself "stuck" in life or in your career, feeling as if you have no direction? Do you worry about people you love eventually leaving you? Does this fear cause you to hold back from fully investing in a relationship now?

4. Are there any specific relationships that you have had or have now that you can connect with the loss of your dad?

5. Please draw a family portrait with your non-dominant hand.

6. Describe your view of God.

7. What does Jeremiah 31:3 have to say about God's attachment to us?

CHAPTER 3

Boundary-Buster Dads

She seems like a normal, ordinary little girl just like me," I thought to myself as I gazed from my observation post atop my mother's washing machine on the back porch. "I wonder if she would like a friend. She looks kind of lonely because she's new in the neighborhood. It would be fun if we could play together and become best friends." My curiosity and anticipation mounted as I climbed down from my perch to investigate the possibility of a new playmate to ease my boredom and loneliness.

I ventured across the field that served as our family's garden in the springtime and cautiously crossed my aunt's neighboring yard, coming to stand across the dirt road from my new target of friendship, Angie. At least that's what she shyly told me when I asked her name. I later found out her full name was Angela Bennett. She also told me when I asked, that yes, she would like to play. But I noticed even then how she cast a furtive glance back to her house as she agreed to help me build a sand castle in the white sand that was so plentiful along the dirt roads of Florida. That was the beginning of a twelve-year friendship that had its ups and downs, cat fights, and daydreams.

Angie and I were inseparable during the summers of our child-hood. We played together, sang together, formed "girls only" clubs, planned birthday parties for her and her brother, and attended Vacation Bible School at her church. She wasn't allowed to attend VBS at my church, because her parents didn't let her do too much or go places with friends. We mostly spent our time at her house because of her parents' rules and control over where she went. I didn't really mind spending all our time at Angie's house. I thought life was boring at home. There wasn't much communication in my family. My mom occupied herself either doing housework or locking herself in her bedroom if she was mad at my dad. To an only child who was lonely, talking and playing at Angie's house at least helped to pass the time in those long, humid Southern summers.

Our days together were fun until Angie's dad came home from work. I tried my best to avoid those times. Mr. Bennett was harsh and mean to Angie. If I was there with her, I felt as if I were in trouble along with her for whatever minor infraction she had committed. Don't get me wrong, Angie was a good girl. I mean a really good girl. She didn't dare breathe loudly around her father, or he would take his rough day at work out on her.

I can still hear the slap of the belt hitting her legs and back as I hurried out the back door of her house and ran to my own. It wasn't that Angie did anything to deserve the physical beatings or verbal tongue lashings she received—she hardly moved for fear of incurring her dad's wrath and another beating when he got home. Her mother seemed to be of little support. She was as strict and cold as Angie's dad, but left the physical beatings to him. One sure way to get her dander up, though, was for Angie's little brother to fall and hurt himself while we were all playing together.

Jim was their darling. If he got hurt or cried, heads would roll, and it was usually Angie's, or sometimes even mine. Though Mrs. Bennett never struck me physically, she angrily blamed me for one of Jim's innocent scrapes on more than one occasion. I'll never forget how ashamed I felt as she threatened me with banishment from her house if Jim got hurt under my watch again. My ten-year-old mind had a hard time comprehending how I was to blame for Jim's riding his tricycle down the porch steps, but I took the blame anyway and ran home crying. I wisely stayed away from Angie's house for several weeks until I was sure that spell had blown over and Angie's mom could tolerate me again.

Years later during graduate school, I realized that Angie grew up in a physically and mentally abusive home. The signs were there, but as a kid I didn't realize it. To us from our youngster point of reference, this was normal behavior. This was how families lived together. At that time, I just filed these experiences under the label of "strict parents." Angie and I didn't really talk about it, except to try to figure out how we could stay out of her dad's way so he wouldn't get mad at us. But one day when I was in fourth grade I realized how the strictness was taking its toll on Angie.

Angie was in a different fourth grade classroom from mine, and had borrowed a book of mine that I needed back. Though I had asked her several times if I could have my book back, she continued to ignore my requests. One morning when Angie's mom was driving us to school, I kept asking. Finally, Mrs. Bennett told Angie to give the book to me and not to borrow anything from me again. Angie angrily swung the book at the side of my face, knocking me against the car door and injuring my eye. Mrs. Bennett irritatedly told us to stop fighting, but chose to ignore my whimpering about my eye.

Upon arrival at school I ran one way and Angie ran the other. I showed my teacher my eye, which by now was swollen and forming a blood clot in the corner. She immediately went to Angie's classroom to tend to the matter. Though I had a good-sized shiner for two weeks, neither Angie nor her mother appeared to notice my injury or apologize for the incident. My mother didn't drive, so I continued to ride to school with them every day. Nobody said a word to me or about the situation. My mother was angry that Angie had been allowed to get away with hurting me, but passively suggested I just keep quiet on the way to school for awhile. Finally, after a period of time passed, Angie and I started talking again and the incident was forgotten.

Years later as a teenager, Angie was shy and insecure about dating. She was hardly ever asked out because her parents were so strict. She learned early on just to say a polite "No" to any invitations for sleepovers with friends or double dates with guys. While I attended dances and football games, Angie stayed home. Finally, as high school seniors, she and I went out on one double date with two classmates. She had a good time, but seemed afraid to enjoy herself for fear of not being allowed the freedom again. Within a year after high school Angie met and married a man much older than herself. They often lived with Angie's parents because Hal, her husband, frequently didn't have a job.

However, more important than home and family provision, Hal was approved by Angie's father. He treated Angie just like her father did, ordering her around to serve him and verbally abusing her if she didn't do exactly as he said. Angie's first child was stillborn. I still remember visiting her afterward in her parent's home. Her body was still swollen from her pregnancy and her eyes looking lifeless, but again she did not talk about the problem at hand. Looking away and not meeting my eyes, she focused instead on making small talk rather than dealing with her internal wounds. Though I was sensitive to her pain and confused by her father's actions, I still did not realize how violated she was. At that time, we were both in denial.

Later on in my graduate training, I realized that as Angie's father trespassed and violated her physical boundaries by beating her, he also trespassed the invisible emotional and mental boundaries of her personhood. By over-controlling her comings and goings and isolating her from other people, he crippled her mentally and emotionally so that she would not think for herself or even entertain the notion that she had the capability or right to think for herself. Thus, she was left dependent on him alone and, therefore, would never leave him. He undermined her personal rights and autonomy in order to keep her a prisoner to do what he wanted.

NORMA

Other fathers, like Norma's, can violate personal, physical boundaries in a different way in order to keep their daughters a possession or object for their own use. "I grew up believing that I was the only one with this problem," Norma shared tentatively. "I've never told anyone, because I was afraid people wouldn't believe me, much less understand. I remember hearing my father say to me over and over again, 'No one will believe you, if you say anything. So don't say a word—if you do, I'll have to go to jail, our family will be destroyed, and it will be all your fault.'

"I really did believe it was all my fault. In the back of my mind I was convinced that somehow I had asked for it. I felt sure this didn't happen to other girls. After all, my dad was a deacon in our church. We attended church every Sunday and Wednesday, he was an usher taking up the offering, and he was always ready to give a hand to a family down on their luck. Who would believe me, a kid, over this ideal Christian father? So I just kept quiet and pretended I was a different person when he crawled into bed with me at night for our special time.

"It all started so gradually and innocently; I didn't see what was coming until it was too late. I remember the first time it happened. It's kind of like a snapshot in my mind. I had almost fallen asleep. But when I felt his hand inside my underwear, I jerked away, saying, 'Dad, I don't like that! Don't do it anymore.' He promised me he wouldn't and quietly crept out of the room. He never kept his promise. It happened again . . . and again.

"When I was twelve and started developing physically, Dad became very jealous. He didn't let me have boys as friends. They could not call me more than once, and he made sure they didn't. Whenever I talked to a boy on the telephone, he went to the extension and rudely interrupted our conversation, saying 'I'm expecting an important call. This is not a convenient time for you to talk.' Needless to say, the boys never called back.

"One friend, Kevin, worked up enough courage to come to my house. Boy was that a mistake! Dad met him at the door and told him I wasn't home. Later, he made sure we had our 'special time' together saying, 'Boys are only after one thing. I'm just trying to protect you.' Feeling confused, I remember asking, 'Then, why is it all right for you to do these things to me?' That's when he told me that it was the responsibility of a good father to introduce his daughter to sex. I wanted to believe Dad really loved me and that I was his special princess. Now I realize that I was just an exploited toy to him."

Grooming techniques of fathers who are sexual abusers often take place so slowly and subtly that childhood victims never notice the boundaries of their personhood have been trespassed until it's too late. This is because boundaries are a learned awareness. Human beings aren't born with self-awareness or a sense of self concept.

During the early weeks and months of life an infant comes from a place of being one with the world to a place of realizing he or she is an object in that world. The most fundamental physical boundary between us and the outside world is our skin. Physically speaking, skin is where we end and others begin.[1] When my skin is touched by another object or person, they have now entered my personal space. We have an inborn right of occupancy to our physical and personal space. We own it, and if others cross it, it should only be done with our permission.

Other boundaries are not so physical or visible, yet they exist. What about my mind or my mental well-being? Don't we control what goes into our minds to a large degree? Indeed, the Bible tells us in Romans 12:2 that we are to be transformed by the renewing of our minds. This implies the responsibility we have for our mental boundaries. What goes past those invisible mental boundaries to feed into our minds comes by way of our choices or others' choices for us.

We also have invisible emotional boundaries on our sense of personhood. Cutting remarks, name calling, and even lack of attention on the part of others, are examples of actions that "hurt our hearts" or cross those invisible boundaries to violate our personhood. We have spiritual boundaries as well. Look at the example of Jesus in Revelation 3:20: "Here I am! I stand at the door and knock. If anyone hears my voice and opens the door, I will come in and eat with him, and he with me." Jesus recognizes the boundary of our hearts. He doesn't "force" Himself on us past the door of our personhood. He knocks first and waits to be invited in. This is a beautiful model of respect for our personhood that God, our own Creator Father provides.

As you see in the diagram on the next page, violations to these boundaried areas can have lasting implications on our personhood unless they are repaired.

Normal Personhood   Impaired Personhood

It is helpful to think of these invisible boundaries as fencelines. Boundary-buster dads, or anyone else who trespasses past these physical, emotional, mental, etc., fencelines can leave our sense of personhood broken. Gaps with needed pieces of ourselves appear. Children of boundary-buster dads are especially prone to these broken fencelines, because dads and moms are our earliest experience of interaction with the world outside our personal boundaries. Parents are entrusted by God to oversee their children's educational process with the world. They are the first ones to teach their children what it means to interact with that world outside the fenceline. If dads interact with their children in physically, verbally, or emotionally abusive ways, they break down those invisible fencelines.

LEARNING TO DANCE THE THREE-STEP

Children who are victims of boundary violations can learn a specific pattern of relating with others. Counselors call this relationship dynamic triangulating. Triangulating relationships always involve three people, instead of two, even in exclusive two-party relationships like marriage. Though triangulation is a frequently observed coping style, it most notably occurs in abusive families where bondaries are violated. For a visual picture of triangulation and how it compares to a normal family dynamic, see the diagram on the next page.

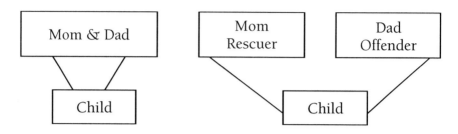

The child becomes caught between the abuser and a would-be rescuer. Physically incestuous fathers triangulate their daughters by intentionally, albeit subtly, reversing the roles of spouse and daughter. They relate to their daughters as they would or should to their wives, thereby breaking down their physical, mental, emotional, and even spiritual boundaries.

However, boundary-buster dads who don't actually violate their child's physical boundary can still violate their invisible emotional boundaries utilizing triangulation. Triangulating of this type invades the child's emotional well-being through dependence on the child to meet the father's emotional needs. Often this dependence is expressed directly and verbally by the father so that his daughter becomes confused about her responsibilities to her father. However, some dads act this dependence out rather than verbalizing it. He may spend more time alone with his daughter than his spouse, actually preferring the daughter's company to that of his spouse. If he puts it into words he may say something akin to "You're the only one in this family who really understands me. I can't really talk to your mother about how I feel. You're easier to talk to." Thus, these dads set their daughters against the mothers, telling them how neglectful their wife is, how they need the daughter to love them and take care of them because their spouse won't.

This type of triangulating puts the daughter in a very difficult position and robs her emotionally of her childhood because she believes she must carry the burden of taking care of her dad. Triangulating of this sort results in what is commonly referred to as emotional incest. While no inappropriate physical touching takes place, the child is still robbed of her place in the family and thrust into the responsibility of being a caretaker of the adults in that family. Emotional incest can also occur among divorced families after Dad has left, when Mom looks to her oldest son to meet her emotional needs. At this point, the son can be violated by Mom as the result of a missing-in-action dad, which we discussed in the last chapter. Either way, sons and daughters can end up father-wounded through emotional incest.

Physically abusive fathers, like Angie's, violate their child's physical boundaries, leaving them hypervigilant about physical relationships and touching. Boys who are physically abused by a boundary-buster father do not learn appropriate self-control for their emotions. They may go on to physically abuse their own children, become a physical batterer of women, or become over-controlled in their emotional expression so they appear robotic and emotionless to others. Both of these extremes of physical expression of emotions can spring from childhood physical abuse. But right now let's take a closer look at how "learning the three-step" (triangulating) in childhood leads to later interactions in adulthood.

Remember the triangle diagram. There were three basic roles—offender, victim, and rescuer. Let's look closer at these roles:

OFFENDER: Offenders are individuals who consistently and characteristically place their needs ahead of someone else, even to the point of exploitation, violation, and physical pain. It usually doesn't matter who they have to step on as long as their emotional and/or physical needs get met. Childhood victims can even turn to offender behavior as a way to compensate themselves for previous feelings of vulnerability and powerlessness. Offenders use power and control inappropriately and ride roughshod over others as a way of making themselves feel power over their own inadequacies and insecurities. Trying to make up for their own perceived childhood neglect, they push and bully their way through the perceived enemy lines of their present families to exploit and offend others as they were once offended.

VICTIM: A victim is a child or individual who has been set up very early in life for exploitation. These individuals have been placed in the middle between the offender and a potential rescuer (usually Mom). The offender leads the three-step by placing the child in the middle between the two parents. This inevitably leads to a breakdown in the child's sense of emotional safety and trust, which in turn leads to broken boundaries. As adults, these broken boundaries manifest themselves usually in one of two ways. Victims can see potential offenders and persecutors everywhere in all domains of their lives and therefore become hypersensitive to the point of paranoia. As they see it, it's them against the world! Spouses, bosses, even their own children in some cases can be perceived as persecuting them. Hurt becomes connected with offendedness. Therefore, if they feel hurt by someone's remark, they will perceive themselves as being violated.

However, some victims of childhood boundary violations may have not yet reached a level of self-awareness that acknowledges they were offended by trusted loved ones early in life. What do they look like? They often continue to become the victims of multiple and repeated instances of physical, sexual, and/or emotional boundary violations such as sexual assaults, date rapes, or physical battering, or they may marry individuals with addictive problems.

If victims can actually acknowledge that their boundaries have been violated, they are on the road to healing. Still, care must be taken that a chronic victim mindset does not become set in place. Better boundaries should result in good choices of relationships with safe people rather than compulsively seeking out people who exploit them.[2]

RESCUER: Victims of boundary-buster dads are often not adequately protected by trusted family members, such as mothers. Due to this inadequate protection and nurturing, they will experience deep emotional neglect and deprivation. As adults, they often discover that by nurturing others, protecting them, or enabling them, they can achieve some vicarious sense of knowing what it's like to be loved and protected. By not having a good sense of boundaries, they may not perceive when enough nurturing takes place. If a little is good, more must be better! Therefore, they can become compulsively addicted to getting their own nurturing needs met vicariously through over-nurturing, over-protecting, over-enabling, and ultimately over-controlling situations. There is an important paradox that often takes place when children are victimized by trusted fathers. Victims of abuse can very often move out of one role in the triangle into another role, once they learn the three-step of triangulation in childhood. Rescuers and offenders can often be untreated victims in disguise!

As a child, you may not have even realized anything was missing after those trespasses over your fence line. But the father who trespasses over his children's personhood creates brokenness in that child. This is a set-up for future boundary trespasses, either by him or others. As children, we don't always understand or perceive accurately because our minds are not developmentally mature enough to comprehend violations. Remember, children can be pretty concrete and often believe boundary violations are normal, because Daddy did it. With no defined limits to themselves, it becomes difficult to tell others "No." Furthermore, children with insecure boundaries often grow into confused adults who do not know who they are and attempt to define themselves by the demands or roles they play. If their invisible fence line is left broken and unrepaired, he/she can find it very difficult just to be a person without some external, defining cue.

Children of boundary-buster dads often become overly dependent on the world to tell them who they are and are frequently set up to be misused and/or violated over and over again. Consider the case of George.

GEORGE

George was raised in a Christian family. His parents were missionaries and George lived part of each year with his family and the other part of the year in a Christian boarding school. Even from a tender age, George had a soft and tender heart. He was an eager learner and helper. His parents held him in high esteem because he seemed to want to follow in their footsteps and go into ministry helping others. George was always very responsible, whether it was schoolwork, babysitting his siblings, or playing on his school soccer team. Everyone could depend on George to pull his load, plus part of someone else's.

George's dad was very busy in the ministry they had in China, but he always had time for his oldest son's spiritual questions. He taught George to be selfless and always to give of himself for others, because this is what Jesus had done on his behalf. George's dad was a great evangelist and loved winning souls for the Lord. During the summers back home with his family and away from school, George labored beside his dad building their ministry. It was no surprise that upon finishing high school George wanted to go on to Bible college and study to be a pastor just like his father.

Ten years later, after finishing Bible college and working as a youth pastor for a few years, George lost his job. The church staff had been cut back due to declining attendance and George's position was temporarily eliminated. With his parents still on the mission field, George had to get through this tough time on his own. He became depressed and questioned God's plan for his life. He felt rejected from the only kind of life he had ever known. He had been taught to selflessly give to build up God's kingdom. But now he felt useless and abandoned by God. Though his father had poured God's Word into his son and taught him to help others, he hadn't taught his son who he was in God's eyes. At his lowest point, George saw himself defined by his slave efforts rather than by God's seal of chosen identity in Him. By allowing him to reach the end of his own resources, ABBA God began to rebuild George into His image, defined not by his performance but by his adoption and sonship into God's kingdom.

Spiritual abuse is every bit as subtle as sexual or mental abuse and every bit as deadly. It is God's desire that the fence line of our personhood in His kingdom not be defined by our works on His behalf, but by our faith in His Son. We are created in His image to do good works, not as proof of our validity, but as a reflection of His working through us. Laboring in the kingdom in order to define ourselves to ourselves is misleading and ultimately leaves us empty, devoid of meaning. Families and churches that teach us to validate our worth in Christ by our works or performance, either through word or example, practice spiritual abuse, often unintentionally. Trying to prove ourselves to God and others is confusing and misleading to us and to others who look to find God through us. Sometimes what they find instead are exhausted and depressed children trying to prove themselves to God. Inevitably this leads to a skewed picture of the One from whom they seek eternal acceptance and approval.

Individuals who suffer from boundary violations at the hands of their fathers often end up with a picture of God that depicts him as unloving, distant, uninvolved, and uncaring. They often have greater difficulty putting painful experiences into a meaningful framework for life that they can learn from.

As a matter of fact, where is God in all of this? What's His position on violation and suffering? "Where was God when I was being violated?" or "Why did God allow this to happen to me?" are the frequent refrains I've heard from individuals struggling with boundary violations to their mind, body, and spirit.

Understanding why God allows pain, evil, suffering, and violations to the innocent is a difficult issue with which to grapple. In our pain, our emotions can color and distort our perceptions of God, making it difficult to see Him accurately. When bad things happen to good people, God's omnipotence and sovereignty clash harshly with our painful realities. We can fantasize Him as being similar to the U.S. President signing and vetoing bills. He examines each potential natural occurrence to see if it has use or purpose. Then He either allows it to happen or vetoes it by divine intervention. The problem with this fantasy is that it takes God's sovereignty and omnipotence out of context of His total attributes and gives us a convenient whipping boy for the moment. Strangely, it doesn't seem to help our pain or make it go away. Indeed, it often increases our sense of hurt and abandonment by God, because blaming God distances us from feeling safe with the only One who can really help us carry our pain.

Rest assured, you are in good company if you have ever struggled to understand God's role in suffering. Just sit down and read the book of Job in the Bible. Job tried to understand it. But he and his friends only added to his misery before they truly understood God's answers. Job's wife tried to help in her own way. Her answer to all of his losses at the hands of God was, "Curse God and die!" Bless her heart, you just have to like her because she's so real! You don't have to wonder how she's dealing with God. At least she's up front and honest about the pain she's in, which is more than we often are at these crucial times of struggle. Consider the questionable accuracy and comfort of these perspectives on violation and suffering offered by Job's friends and ours:

> "God is trying to teach you something. You should feel privileged, not bitter, about your opportunity to lean on Him in faith."

"Meditate on the blessings you still enjoy—at least you are alive. Are you a fair-weather believer?"

"You are undergoing a training regimen, a chance to exercise new muscles of faith. Don't worry—God will not test you beyond your endurance."

"Don't complain so loudly! You will forfeit this opportunity to demonstrate your faithfulness to nonbelievers."

"Someone is always worse off than you. Give thanks despite your circumstances."

Now, each of these pearls of wisdom contains a small element of truth. Many even have scriptural support. And many of them were also uttered by Job's friends. However, as Job found out, none of these answered his questions regarding his personal suffering. Many contemporary writers have struggled with life's sufferings as Job did. Rabbi Kushner, in his landmark book *When Bad Things Happen to Good People*, concludes that "it is too difficult even for God to keep cruelty and chaos from claiming innocent victims. But could man, without God, do it better?"[3]

I tracked with Kushner pretty well until I reached his conclusion that God is powerless. I don't know about you, but the idea that God is powerless in the face of sin and violation not only leaves me anxious, I believe it is a complete lie foisted on us by hell! This lie begs the question: "If we can't blame God for our pain and we can't excuse Him through powerlessness, just what do we do with Him? Just who is responsible here?"

Philip Yancey provides a much more satisfying and biblically accurate solution to God's role in suffering in his book *Disappointment with God*. First, we all need to understand that we live in a fallen world, one in which the innocent sometimes get violated. We cannot confuse God with life.[4] If we have experienced undeserved trauma or injustice in life, it isn't a sign of sin in our lives or a divine message from God to "shape up or ship out." Instead, undeserved suffering exists as a consequence, a natural outgrowth, of a terrible misuse of God's greatest gift to man—the power of choice.

Because we live in an imperfect world due to the fall of mankind outlined in Genesis 3:1-19, we delude ourselves if we expect everything in life to be fair or predictable. Many wrongs will never be made right this side of heaven. God will set the record straight one day. "It is mine to avenge, I will repay," says the Lord in both Deuteronomy 32:35 and Romans 12:19. Until then, we must accept the fact that at times our human experience this side of heaven in a fallen world will be painful and imperfect. Our boundaries will be busted, our fence lines mangled, and our minds twisted. Sometimes we will have heartaches and long-term results to violations imposed upon us. All of this comes from living in a fallen world.

At the same time God promises us in Romans 8:28 "All things God works for the good of those who love Him," or consider the popular paraphrase, "Things work out best for those who make the best of the way things work out."

Now some of you may look at this whole idea of God using pain for good to say: God works pain and joy, good and evil into my life for my good. Thus He allowed me to experience this pain or violation in order to accomplish good. I propose a slightly different twist: God doesn't inflict pain on us to work a certain "good" or growth into our lives. Instead, our lives are touched with the pain of human experience at different points, whether we are Christian or not. In the process of experiencing this pain and walking it out, hand in hand with God, intimacy is built into our relationship with Him. As our closeness with Him increases, growth occurs.

Philip Yancey points out that the great philospher Kierkegaard said that Christians reminded him of schoolboys who want to look up the answers to their math problems in the back of the book rather than work them through.[5] Like Yancey, I confess to a schoolboy mentality at times. I want shortcuts, especially through painful times. I want to know how God will work a situation out before I even go through the situation. We live in the "cyberspace" generation after all! We have access to all kinds of answers anywhere in the world with a keystroke or two! But alas, the easiest road to growing up in Christ is not through shortcuts or keystrokes. Yancey quotes Rabbi Abraham Heschel, stating, "Faith like Job's cannot be shaken because it is the result of having been shaken."[6] Thus Yancey concludes,

"Paradoxically, the most perplexing, Job-like times may help "fertilize" faith and nurture intimacy with God. The deepest faith, what I have called fidelity, sprouts at a point of contradiction, like a blade of grass between stones. Human beings grow by striving, working, stretching, and in a sense, human nature needs problems more than solutions."[7]

Must we have neat and orderly explanations for suffering and being violated by others? The answer is obviously, "No." However, it would appear that the meaning or value of why we suffer injustices comes not by way of an absolute answer from God, but rather the value lies in the struggle and the search for meaning. As I have struggled and pondered my way through trials and violations, I have often been impressed anew with God's grace and provision to me. If left to my own foresight and self-determined direction, I could so easily self-destruct and give up. At various times though, God by His choice (not my direction) reaches out of heaven and intervenes on my behalf, saving me from my own calamities or the mistakes of others. He doesn't do this because it is His job to rescue me. Rather out of His grace and love for me, He gives me at times what I don't deserve—another chance.

As human parents we grant grace and second chances to our children daily. Though our children often expect second chances time after time, as parents we pick and choose when they are appropriate. In the same vein, God doesn't *owe* me a rescue every time I am offended by life. When I take His grace for granted, I lose perspective and simply add to my pain. He is not a vending machine in the sky that if I say the right word or have the right attitude, He will grant me a rescue from life.

However, I do have a different choice of perspective. I can choose to draw wisdom from these divine rescues and make better choices in the future. God and life are different. Because He loves me, my heavenly Father uses life circumstances to help me avoid pain in the future. He doesn't have to do that. He does it because He's my Daddy.

CHAPTER THREE

Group Study Questions

1. Have you experienced abusive fathering? If so, how?

2. What father wound symptoms can you identify in your own life?

3. How does Romans 12:2 instruct us to control our mental well-being?

4. How does Jesus show respect for our personal boundaries in Revelation 3:20?

5. Do you experience gaps in any of your fence lines?

6. How do you practice the "three-step" of triangulation in relationships? Identify who is the victim, offender, and rescuer in each of your situations.

CHAPTER THREE

Homework Questions

1. Recount any early experiences you have had of the following abuses by your father:

   Physical abuse:

   Sexual abuse:

   Verbal Abuse:

   Spiritual Abuse:

   Emotional abuse:

2. What feelings do you have regarding these boundary violations? Do you feel cut off or "numbed" to these experiences?

3. What kind of support or protection (if any) did you receive from other family members? Discuss your feelings about this support or lack of it.

4. Do you behave in compulsive ways to help take care of feelings such as eating problems, substance abuses, workaholism, codependency, sexual addictions, or serial relationships?

5. Do you have difficulty with legal authorities or authority figures at work? If so, what kind of problems have you experienced?

6. Are you presently in an abusive relationship? If so, describe what goes on and name it correctly, i.e. emotional abuse, verbal abuse, etc.

7. Have you acted on any patterns of abuse with your own children that were inflicted on you when you were young? How? Alternatively, do you go overboard and indulge your children in order not to abuse them? Prayerfully commit these patterns to God for change.

8. How comfortable are you with your own sexuality? Try to be as specific as you can. God can handle the truth. How open are you with your spouse about your sexual feelings, desires, and thoughts? Do you desire greater emotional intimacy with your spouse?

The Critical Dad

The sun fanned the field mercilessly. The nine-year-old on the pitcher's mound stepped off momentarily to remove his hat and wipe his brow. Two outs down and one to go in the bottom of the third inning with a full count on this batter. Though his team was ahead, I could tell that Bobby Jordan took nothing for granted, even now. He'd had six strikeouts so far in the game, but he knew now was not the time to let up. You could never let up.

My quiet observance of Bobby's stress-filled demeanor on the mound was in distinct contrast to the response directly behind me two bleacher rows up. There sat Bobby's dad, Tom Jordan, hardware store owner, and all star wannabe. His critique of Bobby's performance ricocheted out to the pitcher's mound and back, making the hair on the back of my neck stand straight up.

"Come on, Bobby. Get the lead out. This guy's an easy out. What are you waiting for, Christmas? C'mon, pull the trigger now." Tom Jordan clipped out the words like rapid-fire bullets.

I kept my eyes fixed on Bobby. He hung his head even lower onto his chest as he replaced his hat on his head. Finally, he looked up at the batter who eyed him uncertainly. Bobby took a step up on the mound, put the ball into his glove, stretched back and threw.

"Ball four. Take your base," the umpire bellowed. I watched as Bobby caught the ball from the catcher and wrung it in his glove while he paced the mound. Meanwhile, Tom had descended the bleachers to give Bobby a "pep-talk" as a new batter grabbed his batting helmet and emerged from the opposing dug-out.

Tom paced the home team fence line yelling at his youngest son, "What has gotten into you, Bobby? Are you tired, or are you a sissy? You know this team has nothing. Why are you letting them get the best of you? Now, get up on that mound and do your job, do you hear me?" Tom screamed, so red-faced I thought surely he was going to have a heart attack.

Bobby's mouth tightened discernibly as he stepped up on the pitcher's mound. I could hear Tom going off again. "Put the ball in the strike zone Bo-bee," he yelled as Bobby let the ball fly.

"Strike," the ump called and the bleachers around me came to life. "That's the way, Bobby," Celia Jensen yelled. "You can do it!" yelled another teammate's father. But the encouraging words for his son were lost on Tom, who continued to pace and shake his head.

Relief coursed through my veins as I saw my husband, Bobby's coach, come around the back of the home team dugout and walk up to Tom. Rocky put an arm around Tom and said as graciously as only he could under the circumstances, "Tom, look at the scoreboard."

Snickers broke out in the home team bleachers as reality hit poor old Tom, 10-0, our favor. Ever the diplomat, Rocky once again had corralled Tom Jordan before he absolutely came unglued and went off altogether on his youngest son. Unfortunately, all of us knew that the truce was only temporary.

As sure as anything, Bobby would hear a blow-by-blow critique of his pitching all the way to the car after the game, all the way home, and probably until he fell asleep from exhaustion. We had all watched Tom Jordan for too many years. First, it was his oldest son, Jack who received Tom's critiques. Finally, one day, after he'd heard enough, Jack walked off the pitcher's mound permanently. Eventually, he dropped out of school and got a construction job. He never came around his dad or the baseball field again. It was a shame, too, because Jack had such potential, but Tom tore it away, shredding Jack's self-confidence year after year.

Tom Jordan had a daughter, too. Jenny played soccer instead of baseball. Soccer was one sport Tom didn't play, but that didn't stop him from coaching Jenny from the sidelines. One day when she was eleven and her dad chewed her out after a game, she too walked away and never looked back. Though she managed to stay in school, she and her father were never close. Jenny avoided going home whenever she could.

Sadly, I saw Tom now on the brink of losing his youngest child, Bobby. By trying to live out his unrealistic dreams for himself through his children, Tom was managing to destroy not only his own children, but his potential grandchildren as well. Without help, Tom's children would likely use his parenting style, "Motivating by Criticism," with their own children.

Over the years I have seen and heard countless variations of Tom Jordan. One father-wounded group member recounted how her father's unrealistic standards for perfection led him to return her letters to him over the years with penciled spelling and grammatical corrections. Other fathers have wounded with verbal judgments that criticized their children's intelligence, appearance, choices, etc. Particularly tragic are those situations where a father criticizes the child's physical appearance, lack of athleticism, or intelligence, which all factor into how a child comes to view himself. Since these are factors that help establish a child's individual identity, his spirit can be quenched when he realizes he is being questioned or criticized for things he cannot change. Sometimes there's a fine line between offering helpful direction in changing a child's performance and criticizing him for who he is as a person. Sadly, some fathers, like Tom, miss this subtle distinction in their zeal to satisfy their own long-unmet needs for attention and approval.

The common attitude communicated by the critical dad is displeasure with his child. They often compare their children or show favoritism for one child over the other. Unaware of their own deep needs, they project them onto their child, sending the message that the child is unacceptable, when in reality they are actually critical of themselves. By their constant harping judgments, they imperceptibly reveal to everyone around them just how dissatisfied they are with who they are.

As in the case of my own father, these dads can even unconsciously communicate their preference for a child of the opposite sex from their child. Growing up, I often heard my father refer to me with the third person pronoun of "he." Gradually, I came to recognize he was talking about me. Since I had no brothers or sisters, "he" had to be me, and I knew I was a girl. As I grew older, I began to perceive that I wasn't acceptable because I was the wrong gender—I wasn't the boy he wanted.

It's been said that a mother teaches her daughter how to be a woman, but it is the father who teaches her she is a woman. A father's acceptance of the child he has, male or female, smart or slow, attractive or plain, is absolutely essential to that child's forming a positive self-concept.

MIRRORED DISTORTIONS OR REFLECTIONS

As I mentioned in the last chapter, not one of us is born with any kind of preconceived notion about who we are. We learn who we are through our experience with the outside world and the people in it, particularly parents. Sociologists reasoned this idea of reflected appraisal as early as 1912 when sociologist Charles Cooley used a mirror to illustrate the idea that "each of us develops a self-concept that matches the way we believe others see us."[1] Therefore, when we receive affirming, positive pieces of information about ourselves, this leads us to see ourselves as worthwhile. However, if we receive messages from significant others that say something is wrong with us, we don't measure up to expectations, or these significant others display indifference to us, the reflection of ourselves that we see in them is of someone who isn't valuable or worthwhile. A person's self-concept is formed by both the positive and the negative messages received from significant people.

Though a child does not begin to acquire language until approximately two years of age, twenty-four months of messages are housed within that child's computer of a brain. By the age of two, a child has a basic idea of whether he or she is loved and considered valuable by those most familiar. Youngsters acquire these early messages largely through non-verbal communication, such as the tone of voice of the person who speaks to them, how they are handled when picked up, how long they are left to cry. Though the child cannot speak a word, information about himself is being typed into his brain through the moment by moment interactions he has with others.

As children grow and acquire language skills, these reflected messages speed up because now he is getting both verbal and non-verbal feedback. Everyday life becomes a bombardment of messages ranging from "You're so cute," to "What's wrong with you?" These evaluative statements, many of them unintentional, become the mirror by which this child forms his identity. If that child receives primarily negative input, or no input in the case of emotional neglect, he ends up with a skewed picture of himself that may not be based in actual reality.

Though many of us struggle to hang onto what self-concept we have, it can be distorted. Some individuals are raised by overly attentive, affectionate, and doting parents. This gives the child a skewed picture of himself—he is the most important individual in the world and his needs are paramount to anyone else's. A child with a negative self-concept is also working off a distortion of reality. Parents often work off their own distorted self-concepts and intentionally or unintentionally feed false, subjective information to their children. However, whether the self-concept is positive or negative, most people seek out individuals who will confirm their own self-view. This tendency to look for people who confirm our self-concept has been called self-verification. As this concept suggests, "we are often less concerned with learning the 'truth' about ourselves, as we are reinforcing a familiar self-concept."[2]

Working off the distorted feedback of our critical fathers can cause us to lose sight of who we truly are. This leads to what Jeff Van Vonderen calls a "shame-based identity."[3] We suffer from low self-esteem, negative self-concept, and the overall perception that we are inadequate, flawed, defective, and unlovable. The child who is overly criticized and judged develops a "shame grid" through which all words, external circumstances, events, and others' treatment is sifted and screened.[4] Once the critical father's words have been internalized, it's as if the child's inner world is patrolled by an imaginary parent sentry telling her she is bad and inadequate for thinking, feeling, and being the way she is. Everything, whether in word or action, that enters that child's life is experienced as an indictment on her personhood because it passes through the shame grid. After awhile, she becomes her own worst enemy. The critical parent is not even needed to put her down—she can take care of that job by herself.

CHALLENGING THE SHAME GRID

Interestingly enough, our enemy, Satan, is ready to use this shame grid to his best advantage. If he can keep us focused on our wounded, inadequate selves, we are unable to see what God, through Jesus Christ, has created in us. When we are willing to be in a more objective place about ourselves and look to our Creator, He can set us straight about who we are. Scripture says in the creation account in Genesis 1:27:

> So God created man in his own image, in the image of God he created him; male and female he created them.

Theologians refer to the likeness we have to our Creator as the *imago dei*.[5] This is because we are "the climax of God's creative activity" and because we are created in God's image, we possess the essence of God, we are worthy of honor and respect, and have been delegated divine authority to rule over the rest of God's creation.[6] The fall of mankind depicted in Genesis 3 brought about a marring or tarnishing of the *imago dei*, but it was not completely destroyed. Due to the marring effects of the fall, our capacity to see things clearly, accurately, and realistically is confused and distorted. Our capacity to view God accurately and completely is tarnished along with our view of the image of God in ourselves. Most importantly, in our sinful tarnished state, we are unable to please God or to be like Him. According to Romans 3:23, mankind in its depraved or tarnished state will never be reconciled to God. However, God made provision for the fallen image of God by sending the Second Person of the Godhead, Jesus Christ, to restore and redeem us through His one-time sufficient sacrifice for all sin (Rom. 5:18-19). If and when we accept Jesus Christ as our reconciliation to God, our sonship is restored and we are made joint heirs with Christ (Gal. 4:4-7). While restoration to the position of sonship is immediate, the process of restoration to the image of God, known as sanctification, takes a lifetime. However, at the point of reconciliation with God, future glorification for one's restored image of God is assured, and God spends the rest of our earthly days preparing us to assume our rightful and promised position (Phil. 1:6; 1 Thess. 5:23).

Though the doctrine about our creation can seem a bit tedious to wade through, the biblical base it supplies about you and me is foundational to establishing a healthy self-concept that is based on truth rather than distortion! Dr. Larry Day in his book *By Design and in God's Image,* pens his illumination to this truth as follows:

> This simple shift of perspective from Genesis 3 (the sinful fall of mankind) to Genesis 1 (our being created in God's image) changed everything! ...Now I saw with new eyes that Jesus did not die for us just because we were sinners. He died for us because He saw us as people made in God's image.... He saw us as Imagebearers first and sinners second. Jesus didn't die for our sins—He died for us! This shift of my attention from Genesis 3 to Genesis 1 changed my whole outlook not only about my worth but helped me see the worth in everyone I met.[7]

After having counseled many Christians over the years, I know how profound this truth really is in healing our woundedness. Adult children of critical fathers have a great deal of difficulty allowing these biblical truths to move the eighteen inches or so from their brains to their hearts. But oh, what glorious awareness and jubilation comes when they finally get it! To know they are Imagebearers and God's delight is in His handiwork in them, instead of His condemnation upon them because they do not measure up, frees them to respond to God's undeniable love for them. No longer do they have to be subject to the judgments of their past. Instead, once they have been reconciled to God through Jesus, they can take on the mind of God about who they really are, not who the critical father of their past thought they were, but who their Father God says they are.

> He brought me out into a spacious place; he rescued me because He delighted in me.
>
> —Psalm 18:19

For you are a people holy to the Lord your God. The Lord your God has chosen you out of all the peoples on the face of the earth to be His people, his treasured possession.

—Deuteronomy 7:6

But God demonstrates His own love for us in this: While we were yet sinners, Christ died for us.

—Romans 5:8

Getting the mind of God about who we are as His children is one of the critical tasks for the Father-wounded. Paul tells us in 1 Corinthians 13:12 that this is no easy task, but one we will struggle with for a lifetime:

Now we see but a poor reflection in a mirror; then we shall see face to face. Now I know in part; then I shall know fully, even as I am fully known.

God's desire is to be able to spend a lifetime teaching us the depths of His love for us. He promises to stick with us until we get it. He will not give up on us (Phil. 1:6). Until we know Him and understand His ultimate sacrifice to keep His purposed plan for us, we will not understand or love ourselves as His Imagebearers.

CHILDREN LEARN WHAT THEY LIVE

If a child lives with criticism he learns to condemn.
If a child lives with hostility he learns to fight.
If a child lives with ridicule he learns to be shy.
If a child lives with shame he learns to feel guilty.
If a child lives with tolerance he learns to be patient.
If a child lives with encouragement he learns confidence.
If a child lives with praise he learns to appreciate.
If a child lives with fairness he learns justice.
If a child lives with security he learns to have faith.
If a child lives with approval he learns to like himself.
If a child lives with acceptance and friendship he learns to find love in the world.

Dorothy Law Nolte, Children Learn What They Live[8]

We are all the product of our experiences to a large degree and we all possess the marred *imago dei*. If we are to live balanced lives in an imperfect world until our Savior returns, we must focus on God's heart for us and choose to turn off the tapes of our past. Working harder to be the child our earthly father wanted will only lead us to burnout and overachievement. Accepting our earthly father's critical and inaccurate indictment against us will only end in underachieving God's plan for our lives. We can, this day, choose whom we will believe.

"For I know the plans I have for you," declares the Lord, "plans to prosper you and not to harm you, plans to give you hope and a future" (Jer. 29:11).

CHAPTER FOUR

Group Study Questions

1. Was your father critical or judgmental to you or members of your immediate family? Write down as many examples of critical remarks he made toward you as you can recall.

2. How did your father's criticism affect you? Record three incidents where you believe your dad was over-critical of you. Using the Feelings list at the back of the book, identify what feeling states you associate with these incidents.

3. What are the critical self-talk tapes that you carry in your head as a result of your dad's judgments?

4. Did you have to play a part, wear a facade, or act a certain way in order to get your dad's approval? Describe how you had to appear.

5. Do others consider you a critical or judgmental person? Do you criticize your children, spouse, pastor, or leaders, either in person or in private? Are you critical of yourself?

6. Are there situations/incidents in your adult life that you see as directly connected to your father's criticism of you? Describe.

CHAPTER FOUR

Homework Questions

1. Look at the chart below. What are the unmet needs in your life as a result of inadequate fathering?

What I didn't get from Dad that I needed	How I meet this need now	Is this a healthy way to meet this need	Healthier Options

2. Write a letter to your father that you do not give to him. In the letter, describe incidents related to the unmet needs you listed above and the feelings you have attached to them. (Use Feelings list [Appendix B] if you need help with connecting and naming feelings to your experiences.) When you have finished the letter, sit down in a comfortable place and visualize your dad sitting across from you. However, he cannot speak back to you at this time. Visualize a piece of duct tape over his mouth if necessary. Now pour out your heart to him. (This exercise is especially transforming if you do it with a trusted friend, small group member, or confidante who, by their silent presence, can validate your painful experience.)

CHAPTER 5

The Shadow Dad

Well stop there for today, Kathy. Next time I want to hear more about your father. You've hardly talked about him at all. You've had a lot to say about your mom, but where does your dad fit in your story?" asked Virginia, my therapist, at the end of my first session. I quit dabbing the tears in my eyes to stare at her blankly.

"Well, he was....just there, I guess," was about all I could come up with as I sat stupefied at her question. She had stumped me and I hadn't even seen it coming. That day twenty-three years ago, I was so focused on the painful relationship I'd had with my mother that I hadn't even given a passing thought to the role my father played in my childhood. "Why was he so important?" I wondered.

I thought about my dad a lot during the next few weeks. At first I was irritated with Virginia that she would focus on him when I felt so badly about other events in my life. Every time I tried to focus on my father and his role in my life, I came up with another blank. I was getting more frustrated by the day. Why was he so important to my therapist when he obviously wasn't important to me? Or was he?

I thought there was little to know about my dad and me. He was always there in the background when my mother and I had an argument. I actually had very few memories of just him and me. When he was home, he was usually too engrossed in the TV to give us much of his time unless our decibel level got too high and it interfered with his program. Though an only child, I grew up in a close extended family living next door to aunts, uncles, cousins, and grandparents. My first cousins and I grew up together for the first twelve years of my life. It was a good thing, too. Without my extended family, I would not have had a social life. My mother was often depressed and withdrawn. My father, being the sole breadwinner in a traditional family, was working most of the time. But even when we were together, we didn't interact much.

As a baby I developed a life-threatening kidney condition that resulted in long hospitalizations from the age of nine months to about five years of age. The resulting medical bills put quite a bit of financial strain on my father. He was consumed with getting them paid off and getting out of debt. He felt ashamed having to ask for financial help from his own parents to help him meet the mounting bills my illness incurred. As a result, he worked overtime and taught courses at night for years to help him meet these obligations and then accumulate a nest egg should a similar crisis ever occur again. As a result, we spent little time together. I don't remember him seeking me out to have conversations or a relationship. I do remember feeling lucky if he did notice or talk to me.

Though I hardly remember my father as a young child, one of my earliest memories with him is when I was about five and he was walking next door to my grandmother's. "Wait for me, daddy," I remember calling as I ran up beside him and grabbed his hand to walk with him. He snatched his hand from mine as quickly as I had grabbed it. He didn't say anything but just kept walking as I ran to keep up. I couldn't understand why this man, whom I adored, was rejecting me.

My father was an auto mechanic. He eventually became an auto mechanic instructor at the local community college where I grew up. He was especially good with the electrical system in cars. But I don't think he knew how to integrate his masculine identity with a young daughter. A daughter was outside his familiar comfort zone. Later when I was in Driver's Education I had to learn the parts of an automobile engine. He seemed disappointed and frustrated when I stumbled over memorizing the correct names for the different parts and the functions of the different systems. I believe he was deeply disappointed in me that I didn't measure up as his child. Rather than extend himself outside his traditionally masculine comfort zone, he relegated the interacting and parenting to my mother because I was a girl.

I missed out on father-daughter interactions that I desperately needed. There was no affection expressed and no "I love you's" verbalized to me. There was nothing much beyond the basic necessities of life, food, shelter, clothing, and medical care. As a little girl, I actually looked forward to funerals in my extended family, because on those occasions distant relatives hugged and paid attention to me.

Over the next week after that initial counseling session, I realized what got Virginia's attention that first day was the obvious lack of father-daughter connectedness in my life. While Virginia picked up on my obvious loss right away, I was clueless! I was used to the lack of relationship with my dad—who was there, but wasn't there. I thought this was how dads acted. I had normalized my father's lack of involvement as being OK. However, Virginia's initial question started me thinking about how difficult it is to try and describe a nonexistent relationship. It also helped me realize that the volatile relationship I had with my mother functioned as a cover-up to hide the lack of relationship I had with my dad.

There were symptoms over the years that I had a deep father hunger. The yearning in my heart for male approval and acceptance from authority figures led me through many academic and later military achievements. I achieved success as a decorated soldier in a traditional man's world. I went on to graduate school, obtaining a doctorate in psychology. I even taught in a local community college, just like my dad. Not having the emotional security that comes with having an involved father directing, helping, and blessing my life's decisions left a void in my life. I looked to other males to fill that void, hoping I would feel affirmed, worthwhile, and accepted. I stumbled through serial relationships with older boys in adolescence and older men as a young adult that always became familiar transactions of premature sexual activity in exchange for love and attention. I longed for relational stability, someone who could go the distance and not physically and emotionally abandon me.

My father's example of anxiety over finances must have burned a hole deep in my soul even as a young child, sending the message that money equaled happiness and security. My mother even recalls my fearful expressions of anxiety as a five year old when I declared, "Mama, if we don't pay our bills, we'll go to the poor house!" Having money in my house equaled security. But my dad wouldn't allow us to spend any because we might hit another crisis. This left me deeply confused about the value of money and economics. I remember working summers beginning at age fourteen just so that I could have my own money to control.

Things began to change when my heavenly Father came knocking. When I accepted God's direction over my life over twenty-seven years ago, my life took a dramatic turn. While things did not change overnight, from the very beginning, God made it clear to me that I needed the direction in my life that only Jesus' Lordship could provide. He also promised to provide the guidance, stability, and security I so desperately longed for if I would yield to Him. The first few years of my Christian life transformed me outside as I responded to God's direction. However, as much as His Word told me He loved me, I still viewed Him in the same distant way I had become accustomed to viewing my dad. Evidently I wasn't alone in my perspective of God, as I learned that theoretical research supported my early views of God as being a reflection of my own father. Piaget, Freud, and Vergote all theorized that a child's experiences with his earthly parents, especially father, shape his representation of God.[1]

Over the last thirteen years God has managed to break down the distance between us and reshape my perspective of Him into His image only. This fathering intimacy and closeness has changed me on the inside. My earthly father's example was too constricting for Him. God has made it His aim to be an up-close and hands-on Dad in my life. I don't just trust His Word and His direction, I trust Him because He is an active, rather than passive force in my life. His breaking down the distance to get to me reassures me of His continued love and acceptance rather than the abandonment I experienced with my earthly father. When I look at all that God has given to me, I realize how much I needed both a Savior and a Father. Thankfully, God knew this before I did.

78

Over the last twenty-two years of my counseling practice, I've met many women like me. The search to find strong men to fill the void left by uninvolved or emotionally distant fathers is as alive in the lives of women today as it has been for millennia. For individuals who come from traditional families where distant fathers left the relating to Mom, it is easy to deny and pretend we come from functional homes. After all, our dad was physically there. There are many father-wounded people who would give anything to have their father live with them. At least we can say we had a father sitting at the head of the dinner table and sleeping in the same house with us. But those of us who lived with this kind of shadow fathering grow up confused and unconsciously searching for father substitutes.

Dr. Beth Erickson refers to emotionally unavailable fathers as "traditional fathers because they have been socialized to take the roles of good provider and firm disciplinarian. Losses from traditional fathers are perhaps the most subtle and difficult for clinicians to diagnose and for clients to acknowledge. These are the everyday losses that people have difficulty naming because of their daily contact with their emotionally unavailable father."[2]

Having a father who is there physically but not mentally or emotionally is very confusing. He's there and he's not. It is difficult to know where you stand or even identify with someone who is a silent presence in your life. A distant or shadow dad can be physically present in the home while being emotionally inaccessible. They often suffer from workaholism, depression, low self-esteem, or alcoholism. They will consciously or unconsciously work at something, either their job or their addiction, just so they never have to get too close and intimate with family members. These dads can leave their families feeling abandoned though they come home every night.

Denial can run deep for individuals who come from these traditional homes that harbor distant dads. These can be Ozzie and Harriet types of homes where Mom did the parenting and Dad made the living. They look together on the outside, while a deep chasm runs through the inside. Physical needs may be met, but emotional needs go wanting. Because basic physical needs like food, clothing, and shelter are met, a child feels guilty and ashamed for wanting more of Dad.

A parent can take a child's understanding for granted and expressions of love, affection, and affirmation don't happen. This kind of emotional neglect can feed a breeding ground for the insidious germ of deprivation. Whenever a child's emotional needs aren't met, deprivation is perceived. Left unattended, this sense of emotional deprivation is often not satisfied with reasonable amounts of attention, caring support, nurturance, etc. Felt deprivation can cause some individuals with neglectful childhoods to demand undue attention and support as adults. They can cling to others, almost holding them hostage to meet insatiable and unrealistic needs for love and attention. Left unchecked, they become leaky buckets. Whatever goes in runs right back out again. Consequently, they often use their friends and partners up before too long.

Just Whose Job Is It Anyway?

Many individuals believe mothers are the key to meeting a child's emotional needs. Mothers do meet many needs of their children and, hopefully, through meeting these needs responsibly, children learn empathy, sensitivity, and compassion. While developmental psychology talks about the importance of early primary dependency upon a child's mother, a child needs a father to help him explore the world beyond the safety of his mother's protection. As Gordon Dalbey points out in *Healing the Masculine Soul,* a boy at some point must be cut away from Mom's apron strings so that he can identify with his father. "The father's role becomes more important as the usher or mentor who calls the child out and initiates or empowers him to function productively in that world."[3] Wise fathers assume this initiation responsibility and wise mothers rightfully relinquish their sons to this rite of passage. Sons need a father's active, hands-on example of manhood. As much as he may love his mother, a son needs a male to help him assume his masculine responsibilities. Mothers can't give this to their sons. It is only the gift of fathers.

If Dad becomes so involved in earning a living or some other pursuit that he can't see his own child's needs, his son will live under the impression that this is how men act—busy, distant, and uninvolved with their children. This becomes his template for life that will follow him into adulthood as he makes life choices. The evidence to support the necessity of paternal responsibility seems to be everywhere these days, from school shootings to drug use. Just this morning another local newspaper headline looms bearing testimony to this sobering fact: "Study Cites Aloof Dads in Teen Use of Drugs." A study performed by the National Center on Addiction and Substance Abuse at Columbia University reveals that teens who have a poor relationship with their fathers are more likely to smoke, drink, or use drugs. Teen-agers from single parent families, i.e. mothers, were found to be less at risk for drug use than those with unstable relationships with their fathers.[4]

Active fathering can have no respect for gender either. Both sons and daughters suffer when Dad passively allows them to raise themselves. Both genders need active participation from fathers in their lives. Daughters especially need to know their fathers are there, actively communicating his interest in her and teaching her to protect her interests. "The ability of you and your daughter to effectively exchange words—and the feelings they're usually connected to—will provide the bridge between you that will last the rest of your life."[5]

From his example in how he behaves with her, a daughter learns she is worthy of respect and honor. This determines the caliber of men she allows in her life. Without her father's example of respect, daughters are unable to distinguish between sincere and insincere efforts at respect and honor that may come their way. Dads set the standard against which all future suitors will be compared. Security also grows out of knowing Dad, the protector, is always there to back her up if she needs it. Self-confidence and competence at protecting herself is birthed in her conversations with Dad, which help to clarify her values and give her invaluable practice in verbalizing her commitments to purity and respect. When she feels sure of holding her own with Dad, she can hold her own when it comes to choosing between talking and moving to the backseat. Fathers provide the launching pad for both genders. His presence and active participation sets the child's life direction and is responsible for blessing and releasing his child's transition into adulthood. It's as if he gives his child tacit permission to leave the nest and separate from family, and become the adult God gifts him or her to be. If a father abdicates

God's example of responsible parenting to his children by remaining remote, uncommunicative, and non-participating in their lives, both he and his child lose out on fathering future generations successfully. A wise man once said that the proof of fathering isn't in how a man's own children turn out, but in how his grandchildren turn out. This bears a striking resemblance to "A good man leaves an inheritance for his children's children" (Prov. 13:22).

Paul Lewis characterizes this imprint on subsequent generations as a "tire tread."[6] Good, bad, or indifferent, these treads leave a legacy on the souls of the future. Lewis also believes this legacy leaves fathers at a disadvantage in knowing how to father. "This decade is witnessing what may be the first generation of Americans in which a substantial number of dads have grown up without fathers in their homes."[7] If the template is missing or passive, how does a man know how to be a man and a father?

Consider Leanne Payne's synthesis of this generational problem with male role models: "Unaffirmed men are unable adequately to affirm their own sons and daughters as male and female and therefore as persons. Until men are once again functioing in this vital capacity, women will continue to attempt to fill the gap in vain, and will continue to verbalize their pain and confusion."[8]

BACK TO THE FALL

Since the fall of man, all of mankind has had difficulty assuming their God-given responsibilities in life. We see how Adam dealt with responsibility in Genesis 3:12: "The man said, 'The woman you put here with me—she gave me some fruit from the tree, and I ate it." Adam blamed his disobedience on Eve, and ultimately, God. After all, God made Eve. Therefore, it was God's and that woman's fault that he was tempted. Interestingly enough, God didn't see it that way then and I don't think He views women as being responsible for men now, either. Genesis 3:14-20 details that God punished not only the tempter, Satan, but Adam and Eve as well. In particular, he punishes Adam because he listened to his wife instead of following through on the command God had originally given for both him and Eve.

Up until the 1990s not much had changed concerning men's response to God's responsibilities. Church, religion, and family have largely been attended by women through the ages. Most men saw themselves as the traditional breadwinner, but hearth and home were women's jobs. The 1980s were seen as the "decade of the woman," where traditional and patriarchal chains were unloosed so that women could address their emotional needs and realize their God-given potential.

THE DECADE OF THE MAN

The 1990s brought the "decade of the man." In 1992 the National Center for Fathering commissioned Gallup to conduct a study on fathering in America. While seven out of ten adults characterized their relationship with their father in positive terms, seventeen percent described their relationship with their dads in negative terms.[9]

Starting in the mid-1990s, organizations such as Promise Keepers began to call men forth to accept the reins of responsibility for their families and our nation that had long been relinquished to excuses, blaming, and preoccupation with work to meet their emotional needs for worth. The men's movement brought forth male voices that understood the secret emotional needs of men and the struggles they experienced in discovering God's purpose for them as they said, "Let's stand together!"

Many of those men raising their hands and standing up to be responsible men and fathers began in uncharted territory. Many of them had no idea what it was to be a "real man" or a responsible father. They were numb to their pain, with little clarity to the legacy they carried. They didn't have a clue because many were father-wounded themselves. Pastor Ted Roberts nails the source of pain when he says, "The vast majority of men I have counseled who struggle with sexual issues have father wounds in their souls."[10]

I can't help but wonder if the Gallup poll results I just referred to would be the same today, after men have been challenged to assume their masculine responsibilities. When individuals have to accept responsibilities for tasks they feel ill-prepared to assume, they will often look deeper and discover the void within. Denial will break down as they face their felt inadequacy and look to a heavenly Father for a righteous example. This is the first step in healing their father-wounds and becoming better fathers for the next generations.

In the eleven years that I have led father-wound classes and workshops, I have never been so moved as I was a few years ago when I led my first workshop of sixty men in identifying their father-woundedness. Though God had planted the idea of this workshop exclusively for men in my heart, nothing could have prepared me for the humility and compassion I felt rise up within me as I watched sixty men face and tell each other with tears streaming down their faces of their deep-seated father-wounds, losses, and inadequacies. There was not a dry eye in the place, including mine! The Holy Spirit moved healing into many hearts that day because these men had the self-awareness and courage to identify and lay down their hurts before God and each other. Indeed, untouched wounds can sit just below the surface of our awareness. Many times those around us see our symptoms of woundedness long before we do. However, wounded behavior can be detected by the discerning eye. For those who come from traditional homes where denial runs deep, identification of these symptoms is particularly important. For that reason, I have included a list of father-wound symptoms for both males and females. See if any describe you:

Male Father-wound Symptoms

- Consistently overly defensive about mistakes
- Feels inferior and insecure as a man
- Overly controlling in order to cover up feelings of inferiority
- Feels intimidated in the presence of other men
- Uses indirect ways of communicating needs
- Competitive, even in environments that aren't
- Physically and/or emotionally dependent on women in his life
- Serial relationships, out of one relationship into another
- Sexually addicted
- Chemically addicted

The Shadow Dad

- Highly driven in business dealings
- Moves from one job to another, can't find his niche
- Low to zero emotional connection with others
- Workaholic
- Avoids social interactions
- Underfunctions in relationships
- Doesn't form stable attachments
- History of relationships with "controlling" women
- Macho, independent facade
- Feels numb or disconnected from feelings
- Abusive and/or disrespectful to others (physical, sexual, verbal, mental, etc.)

Female Father-wound Symptoms

- Feels insecure as a woman
- Clingy and over-dependent on others
- Driven and counter-dependent
- Overfunctions in relationships
- Uncomfortable with their emotions
- Seeks male attention and approval
- Often feels abandoned by males
- High maintenance—demanding
- Blurred sense of boundaries
- Competency issues
- Manipulative
- Serial relationships
- Substance addiction—chemicals or food
- Under-realized ambitions
- History of relationships with underfunctioning and/or controlling men
- Hypermasculine, counterdependent facade
- Emotionally disconnected from feelings
- Emotionally controlled
- Displaced anger
- Unhealthy attachments to unattachable people

Where are you in your healing? Can you identify three or four of these symptoms that you know in your heart characterize you? That's a good start. You don't have to have more than one or two to be experiencing unsatisfactory relationships and unmet needs. All of us must identify and own the indicators of our woundedness before we can start to heal. I call this the "Name It and Claim It Game." Unlike other name it and claim it philosophies that suggest that just by thinking a certain dream or goal you can make it yours, my exercise is much more painful and self-revealing. By naming and claiming your wounds, you take the first step of responsible healing. Our God is an awesome God, but even He doesn't heal us if we don't know we're sick. Naming and claiming our wounds helps us accept responsibility for the woundedness we bear and the healing we need.

Why is healing so necessary? Healing is required if we are to achieve the closeness with others that God intended from the beginning. Jesus said in John 13:34-35:

> A new command I give you: Love one another. As I have loved you, so you must love one another. By this all men will know that you are my disciples, if you love one another.

God desires that His kids in the kingdom get along with each other until He comes back. He knows that will take the flexibility of grace and love, as well as a lot of spandex! You see, it's much easier to live in denial about our own warts, if the problem is always out there. Coming to grips with our own wounds and how they hurt and impact others is no fun at all. But it can make us realize why we need a Savior. In turn, this ownership of our wounds grows grace in our lives that extends to others and promotes peaceful coexistence in the kingdom until our real Father comes back to get us.

CHAPTER FIVE

Group Study Questions

1. Did you grow up with a father who was inattentive to your emotional needs? How do you remember feeling when he wasn't available to you?

2. In retrospect, did any other family members attempt to meet your emotional needs as a way of compensating for the time you needed with your father?

3. What types of ways did you use to try to get your father's attention and did they work?

4. What are your father-wound symptoms?

CHAPTER FIVE

Homework Questions

1. Do you have a stepfather? If so, how old were you when he came into your life, and how was your relationship with him? Did he try and compensate for your father, or was his behavior worse?

2. Begin talking with extended family members to access their memories of your dad and his relationship with you. It is all right if their memories conflict with yours. Everyone is entitled to their own perspective of events. As you begin to walk down "memory lane" with family members, begin to practice the art of self-monitoring. In other words, tune into you. What feelings do you have attached to these memories? Increase your self-awareness as you reclaim these bits of your past. Although this contact with extended family members may involve writing letters or telephone conversations, it is well worth the effort if it puts you in touch with your historical roots.

3. How was your relationship with your mother, and was it affected by the lack of relationship with your father?

4. Draw the floor plan (in your non-dominant hand of course) of the house(s) or apartment(s) where you grew up. Draw your dad in the room or place that you remember he spent most of his time. Now draw you and where you spent most of your time.

CHAPTER 6

Unlocking Anger's Bondage

MAGGIE

He had no right to ignore me like he did. I was his only daughter. The only time he gave me a scrap of attention was when he wanted me to do some chore for him. I worked hard just to get him to notice me and approve. Now, I'm married to a man just like my father! As long as his dinner is ready at 6:00 P.M. when he comes home and he has clean clothes to wear, he's happy. But I'm not! As soon as he comes home he hides out behind the newspaper, then watches TV until he falls asleep in his chair. I'm living my childhood all over again!" Maggie heatedly finished as her bright blue eyes threatened to spill their pent-up tears. Before I could make a stab at any empathic response, she was off and running again.

"What is wrong with me that I can't get the men in my life to pay attention to me? Do I have to be dying to get them to wake up? And if I hated my father's ignoring me so much, how did I end up with a man just like him? I don't get it!"

Again I tried to open my mouth to speak a supportive word but was forestalled. Maggie's voice was growing shriller by the minute. "I hate men! I can't trust them. Not one of them—my father, brother, boyfriends, or husband—has ever showed they cared about my needs, just theirs. I'm sick to death of it!" Finally, she stopped long enough to blow her nose into the tissue I offered. I seized the opportunity to offer a belated, if not reflective, show of support.

"You're pretty ticked off at your dad, aren't you," sounded pretty lame beside her five-minute tirade. "No male in your life has ever given the love and support you believe you deserve," I finished quietly.

"Yes!" she spat at me with bright blue eyes that shot daggers. "Please explain to me what is so horribly wrong with me that none of them has ever loved me the way I needed to be loved. It's just not fair!"

"I hear a lot of pain in your words, Maggie. For all your fury, there's a ton of hurt feelings underneath, feeding your anger and causing it to burn. Our job together will be to look at the pain and hurt underneath your burning embers," I said.

Maggie's anger and hurt were inextricably bound together. The only way she could be proactive about attending to her hurt was to bottle it in anger. I have seen many individuals get stuck in this angry expression of their pain. For months and years they do nothing but spit and sputter in the same tracks. To their loved ones, they appear as an angry, bitter, resentful, or raging person. Unfortunately, they are often the last to recognize the high price their raging embers may be exacting.

Anger is really only the first line of defense between hidden pain and the threat of being hurt again. What causes the flames of Maggie's anger and others' to burn continuously or rage out of control is not the emotion of anger itself, but the fueling embers of pain, hurt, anxiety, or fear underneath that their anger protects.

Many individuals will tell me in a heartbeat they much prefer a strong presentation of their feelings, even if it is angry, than to be caught in the vulnerable, scared position of letting someone see just how much they really hurt. The angry presentation says, "You can't hurt me anymore!" The hurt or fearful presentation would say, "You might hurt me again terribly." In the face of a perceived threat, which presentation would you prefer? Anger is one way many people are able to hide what they really feel underneath even from themselves.

It is perfectly normal and healthy to feel anger toward your father. You counted on him for support and he let you down. The key lies in ventilating that anger properly so you don't bury it alive or fuel its flame. Practicing either of these unhealthy alternatives will throw everyone off the track, including yourself. By hiding behind the flames of your anger, no one knows how you really feel, least of all you! Save yourself a lot of time, maybe even a few therapy dollars—admit you're angry and search underneath the anger to see what else you

1	2	3	4	5	6	7	8	9	10
irritated, frustrated			angry, upset		heated		enraged		out of control

may be feeling that is closer to your inner core. Some people find it helpful to picture anger on a continuum like the one below:

Truthfully, I find individuals often feel afraid that acknowledgment of their anger will lead to abandonment of others. Is it better to acknowledge you're angry rather than deny it exists and spew it out onto other people who know only too well just how angry you really are! This hurts innocent people and locks us into denial. The next time we feel our anger burning, we need to take a shortcut and search out what's underneath, rather than letting it keep ringing the fire bell!

EMOTIONAL CREATIONS

Children of critical fathers can bear their father's judgmental projections. Consequently, these offspring have difficulty accepting themselves as whole persons having both positive and negative emotions, because their fathers have difficulty accepting them this way. One of the often misunderstood attributes of bearing the image of God is that we, like our Creator, have a tremendous capacity and range of feeling and emotion. God displays emotion! For that matter, so did Jesus when He angrily tossed the money changers out of the temple (Matt. 21:12), when He sorrowfully wept at Lazarus' grave (John 11:35), and when He anxiously begged God to spare Him the pain of the cross (Matt. 26:39). Yet, many of us come from homes where the emotional side of our likeness to God isn't acknowledged. Consequently, Christian adults walk around every day without a clue as to what they feel. Many have been taught that feelings don't exist or are just the fleshly part of themselves that must die. Neither God nor Jesus ever tried to kill their feelings. "God has created the full range of emotional reactions that people have, and each emotion has a purpose. Even those which seem to be destructive or negative, like anger and fear, are intended to be helpful."[1] Feelings and emotions are one of the concrete assurances that we are indeed created in the image of God.

So how have we gotten to such a misunderstanding about the emotional part of our image? Quite likely it has been passed down generationally through the consequences of uncontrolled or exaggerated displays of emotion, i.e. going to prison for murder provoked in part by jealous rage, jail time for domestic violence, or suicide at the hands of a depressed individual. Left unchecked, the emotions of anger and rage can kill and maim. Depression and anxiety can lead to killing oneself. We see the outrageous acting out of emotions like this and our first and natural instinct is to quell or dampen down any emotional response we may have. To keep emotional expression from getting out of control, parents have often said, "Don't feel that way," "It's wrong to hate," or, "Don't get mad about that!" to their children. Unknowingly they have given the child the unspoken message, "Don't feel," or at least, "don't express your feelings." Unintentionally, many parents cut their children off from their emotional experience. The end result is lack of emotional awareness and a disconnectedness from a vital part of our image of God. Though we can fool ourselves by stuffing away our unexpressed feelings, we can never fool God. Feelings aren't expressed and get buried alive.

Our God Is Big Enough

Our God is much bigger in His understanding of His creation than we are. He can handle our emotions and He can handle us. And with a little instruction about how emotions work, we can handle ourselves and our feelings. We do not have to be subject to having our lives run by unexpressed emotions that may have been buried alive. If we learn to be aware and identify how we truly feel, we can take appropriate steps to take care of those feelings instead of acting them out on others. In Appendix B, in the back of this book, you will find two lists of feelings. Use them to help you identify your feeling status and then own your feelings.

In teaching people about their creator-given emotional makeup, I often run into two different extremes of people struggling with self-control. Some people have bought into the "don't feel" message lock, stock, and barrel. Consequently, they are so emotionally over controlled, the most they can admit to feeling is numb. The task for these folks is to begin identifying what they feel by tuning in to their physical reactions, their non-verbal behaviors, or their thought life. These three areas used with the Feelings lists at the back of the book can help an individual better understand how they feel and respond to different situations.

Other individuals realize their feelings haven't been given much validation or attention by significant others. Feeling neglected or unheard, their response is to pay too much attention to what they feel. By overindulging the emotional part of themselves, they give their feelings too much power and control over their behavior and well-being. One of the crucial lessons for these individuals is that feeling and acting are not the same thing.[2] Just because we feel a certain way, does not mean the feeling must control us or our lives. "Neither repressing emotions out of fear nor allowing them to dominate constitutes the scriptural way....God intends to transform people so that their emotions instinctively support them in righteous living."[3]

	Focus on Cues	Feeling & Acting Not the Same	Take Responsibility for Feeling
1. Emotionally overcontrolled	Yes	No	Yes
2. Emotionally controlled	No	Yes	Yes

Both of these emotional mindsets also have one other task in common regarding their emotions—they must learn to take responsibility for what they feel. No one causes us to feel. We do that job all by ourselves. For instance, most everyone agrees that you can't make someone fall in love with you. So if you can't make someone love you, then it also must follow that no one can make you angry, or sad, or mad, or glad, etc. Our feelings and emotions are not externally caused.[4] They occur internally as we respond to others' behavior. Therefore, they are caused by our choices, not others'.

The importance of paying some attention to our feeling cues cannot be overemphasized. Emotional responses can be a first-line alert signaling that deeper, more gut-level emotions are in danger of being discovered or threatened. Anger is one of these primary, first-alert emotions. Anger can function as an emotional boundary line around deeper, more personal and vulnerable emotions such as hurt and fear. Maybe you've noticed this in yourself. If someone calls attention to an error or mistake you may have made, do you automatically (before you can stop it) feel a spark of angry defense? People feel defensive and angry when they perceive a threat to themselves, real or imagined. Their "anger alert" goes off, letting them

know within themselves that more vulnerable emotions are in danger of surfacing. Looking at anger this way, we can see that it serves a useful function rather than just a negative display. Looking at our anger can give us valuable clues as to what we feel deeply about. I think of this function of anger as a healthy protector, much like a guarded fence line around our heart.

Now, I know Christians have a hard time speaking their anger. After all, the last thing most of us want to be perceived as is an angry, out-of-control person. Yet we have a God who got angry at times and we are created in His image. Therefore, our anger is God-given. What often contributes to the bad publicity this God-given emotion receives is the way we manage it or act it out on others, hurting and victimizing them in the process. However, if we turn it back on ourselves, we can experience needless depression and/or physical illness. Acting out our anger on others just to make ourselves feel better is hardly righteous. However, when prayerfully considered and carefully spoken, anger can be managed righteously and can provide necessary energy and motivation toward our goals.

Spirit Control?

As an alternative to being emotionally controlled or emotionally over-controlled, what about being spirit controlled? Galatians 16:26 proposes that we live by the fruit of the Spirit:

> The acts of the sinful nature are obvious: sexual immorality, impurity and debauchery; idolatry and witchcraft; hatred, discord, jealousy, fits of rage, selfish ambition, dissensions, factions and envy; drunkenness, orgies, and the like. I warn you, as I did before, that those who live like this will not inherit the kingdom of God. But the fruit of the Spirit is love, joy, peace, patience, kindness, goodness, faithfulness, gentleness and self-control. Against such things there is no law. Those who belong to Christ Jesus have crucified the sinful nature with its passions and desires. Since we live by the Spirit, let us keep in step with the Spirit. Let us not become conceited, provoking and envying one another.

As I read that passage over and over, I am struck by the number of emotions Paul lists and the actions he ties to those emotions. He is not condemning the emotions, but the behavior patterns these emotions pressure us to act out on one another. Paul reminds us that those of us who have been reconciled with God can now choose to live according to the Spirit of God's urging in our lives.

Keeping in step with the Holy Spirit requires us to know the Image to which we are being conformed. To stay in step we must know and be known by the Spirit so intimately that as the Spirit breathes, so do we.

We are all the product of our experiences to a large degree, and we all possess a marred image that is in the process of being restored. If we are to live balanced, healthy lives in an imperfect world until our Savior returns for us, we must seek our heavenly Father's heart for us, making choices that conform us to the original image. All of this comes with a choice. We can choose to keep listening to the tapes of our past failures, but listening to the programming of our earthly fathers may result in underachieving our heavenly Father's plans for us. However, following the Holy Spirit's lead kneads the desires of our heavenly Father out of our hearts and into our actions. So, expressing our anger may require us to press in and lean a little heavier on Him so as not to give in to our natural desires. This leaning in and following after the Spirit requires submission to His Lordship and a relinquishment of our own ways of understanding a situation.

RELEARNING YOUR ABC'S

We can often labor under the misbelief that others or external situations cause us to feel. As I mentioned previously, this is a false belief. Activating conditions do not cause us to feel certain emotions as a consequence. Despite the fact that our felt reactions can happen in a split second, there are usually beliefs that come into play between the event that activates us and our felt consequences. Let me illustrate it this way: Let's say you are in a rush to get to work one morning. You have a report that's due to your boss by noon, and you still have several pages to finish. On the way to work there's a five-car pile-up that stalls traffic to a crawl for the five miles you have to drive to work. In this instance, you might feel anxious and angry, fearing you won't make it to work in time to finish your report.

Now, let's take the same situation again. This time, however, you do not have a report that is due to your boss by noon. You have some work to do, but it isn't anything that is up against a deadline. There's a five-car pile-up that stalls traffic to a crawl for the five miles you have to drive to work. In this instance, knowing that you do not have a deadline to meet, you might only feel inconvenienced and irritated that the commute is taking so long.

Notice that the activating situation did not change in either scenario: a five-car pile-up that slows traffic to a crawl. However, your feelings changed from anxious and angry in the first scenario to inconvenienced and irritated in the second scenario. What was the difference? The difference lies in what you knew, thought, or believed about the situation. In the first instance you knew you had a deadline, and you may have thought your boss would be brandishing the whip if you weren't right on task every minute. In the second instance, you may have thought your boss wasn't quite so interested in your progress.

Though situations and circumstances can influence our thinking, we often mistakenly give them much more power in our lives by giving them credit for making us feel. Why, we can even attribute negative and volatile feelings to others, laboring under the gross misunderstanding that other people have the power to make us feel certain feelings. As we analyzed the situation of the five-car pile-up, we can begin to see that the problem doesn't lie outside of us in an external circumstance or person, the problem lies between our own two ears in what we think, perceive, or believe about a situation. Relearning our ABC's requires us to put the B back into its rightful location between the A and the C.

activators   beliefs   consequent feelings

It is normal to doubt the truth of this paradigm at first. However, the more we slow down our thought process to examine what we're thinking about that may be influencing our feelings, the more we recognize how our own stinkin' thinkin' may be creating and feeding emotions that seem to control us. Changing our thinking, questioning our perceptions, and challenging our beliefs about situations and circumstances releases us from the bondage of emotional control. Romans 12:3 tells us we are to regard ourselves soberly. Interestingly enough, this verse comes on the heels of Romans 12:1-2 which says:

> Therefore, I urge you brothers, in view of God's mercy, to offer your bodies as living sacrifices, holy and pleasing to God—this is your spiritual act of worship. Do not conform any longer to the pattern of this world, but be transformed by the renewing of your mind. Then you will be able to test and approve what God's will is—his good, pleasing, and perfect will.

Perhaps you're beginning to see the key to unlocking emotional or anger's bondage. The first key lies in the daily action of sacrificing ourselves to Jesus' lordship. As we seek to be led by the Holy Spirit, our minds will be renewed and transformed. In other words, we will think differently. As our stinkin' thinkin' changes, we will experience renewal by the Holy Spirit to recognize God's call to obedience in situations that have previously sabotaged us. The power of unlocking anger's bondage lies in submissively handing over our will and our minds to the Holy Spirit's perfecting work before we act in the flesh.

CHAPTER SIX

Group Study Questions

1. How do you view your relationship with your dad when you look at it from your child's point of view? What did you lack? Name the ways he "actively" hurt you.

2. Are you afraid to truly let go and feel your pain inside? What do you fear will happen?

3. How do you avoid feeling the pain inside? List the ways.

4. Are there behaviors that reveal your inner pains inside? List them.

5. On a scale of 1-10, how angry are you over your injustices and how does it spill out onto people around you? (Remember frustration, irritation, cynicism, sarcasm, contempt, and whining are all examples of underlying unresolved anger.)

6. What examples of anger did you witness as a child?

7. Are there situations in your life where you displayed "constructive anger" even though it may not have turned out well?

8. What are the core emotions that anger protects in you?

CHAPTER SIX

Homework Questions

1. Complete the following statement writing in as many ways as you can to name the feelings and/or situations you struggle with concerning your dad:

   Dad, when you, _____ I felt _____ _____.

2. Choose at least two of the following anger exercises to complete in order to adequately process your feelings of anger so that you can get to the core emotions underneath the anger. These are constructive anger exercises that will help to drain the physical and emotional energy and intensity in yourself and reduce the likelihood that you will project, displace, or transfer this anger onto the innocent people in your life.

   ANGER LISTS: Take out several sheets of paper. Write the following heading at the top: I FEEL ANGRY WITH YOU BECAUSE: Now write as many items of anger on this list as you need to write to empty out your anger reservoir. Each statement has to begin with I FEEL ANGRY WITH YOU BECAUSE. Keep these sheets handy and add items to them as they surface for you over the next week.

   "GET OFF MY BACK!" Visualize the weight of the hurt and suffering you carry from your father laying squarely on your back. Without moving any other part of your body, take your elbow and jerk behind you at shoulder level, while saying, "Get off my back!" Do this as many times as you like while no one else is around.

   PRIVATE SCREAMFEST OR TEMPER TANTRUM: Wait until no one is at home or, better yet, drive out to a field and scream until you exhaust yourself. Or you can get down on the floor of your bedroom and kick and scream through your very own temper tantrum. Then resume having a normal day.

   IT'S A BLAST! Rip out pages from an old telephone directory, ball them up, and throw them while yelling whatever befitting names or expletives you can think of that fit your dad's behavior toward you. This is best if you can fire your "bullets" into a couch, chair, or fireplace. When you have used up all the names you can think of, gather up your "bullets" and go for "rapid fire" telling your dad just what you think.

BEAT YOUR BED! Get a 3-4 foot piece of foam tubing from the hardware store or your child's Nerf bat. Beat your bed with the tubing for 20 minutes. Physical exhaustion is a great release for anger. Make sure you do at least 20 minutes. Do not shortchange your anger's expression so that it leaks onto others inappropriately.

3. Now it's time to prepare your grievance list about your dad. Take stock of what you still resent about your father and/or his behaviors toward you and write down each individual grievance. Keep writing the statement from number one above with different endings until you have exhausted your complete inventory of offenses for which you can't yet forgive your dad. Please do not play games with God or yourself about this exercise. God already knows your heart better than you do. He knows what grievances you harbor. He will probably help you write the list!

CHAPTER 7

· ·

Father Prisms

I held the champagne glass up to the light and scrutinized it carefully. As I twirled it, slivers of light danced off each facet of the delicate cut glass. As I turned the glass, checking for flaws, I marveled at the brilliance each facet of the glass could cast on its own. Because of the intricate cutting procedure of the Crystal Meister, each glass became a story unto itself, reflecting light from several directions at once, providing a kaleidoscope of perspective to the onlooker. And being the novice I was, I could find no flaws in the Crystal Meister's handiwork.

Though these champagne glasses were marked as seconds, the flaws were invisible to the public eye. Shoppers like me snatched these seconds up by the sets, gleeful at our good fortune to come at just the right time as the newest merchandise arrived on the showroom floor.

My friend Connie and I had already spent two days methodically driving and scouring the southern countryside of Germany for crystal and porcelain factories. We went from our home in the southwestern end, clear to the eastern border that ran alongside Czechoslovakia. The back of her little Subaru station wagon already sagged under our purchases from factories large and small that dotted the German countryside.

This trek was to have been my last "hurrah" of shopping the bargains of Germany before I returned to the U.S. after four years of overseas military service. And what a hurrah it had been! Connie and I had talked, giggled, and talked some more as we went up hills, along two-lane country roads, sometimes behind a honey (manure) wagon on its way to a waiting field, and sometimes just behind a German farmer heading home for the day. We had even spent the night at a gasthaus in the middle of a hayfield! Though my sinuses paid the price, the promise of the memories we were making offset the stuffiness in my head.

We had truly found some bargains as we sifted and hunted through sets of dishes, porcelain figurines, glassware, gravy boats, and cake plates to find the hidden treasures that now filled the groaning little station wagon as it huffed up one hill to shoot down the other side, relieved by its temporary respite from work. I was so thrilled with my seconds on champagne glasses that I bought seconds on wine glasses as well! Who cared that I didn't drink anymore since coming to Christ; this was just too good a deal to pass up!

Years later, listening to a sermon by my pastor comparing perspectives of God to a glass prism, I thought of my beautiful champagne glasses lying securely at home in my German china closet. Yes, I could see the analogy of comparing a glass prism to the attributes of God. God took me one step further and suggested I hold my own life up to the light and examine the prism of my experience. He showed me how He moved me through my early beginnings as a sickly child growing up on the white-sand roads of the South, taken me on a world-wide education, forgiven and graced my mistakes and missteps to deposit me across the U.S. in Western Oregon to take part in raising up the next generation. Indeed, my life touched by the Master's hand had facets and cuts to it that testified of a supernatural touch.

In humility, I realized that each human life, not just mine, is shaped in part by the Master's hand. It's true that our own free will serves to carve and etch our direction, but each facet of our lives is Father-filtered, whether we credit God with it or not. As I moved from the narcissistic ponderings of my own life-prism, my thoughts naturally turned to the life-prisms that had influenced mine.

THE OLDEN DAYS

Have you ever stopped to consider that your parents had a life before your existence? I know this is an abstract idea for my own children to grasp. When they are confronted with some fact or truth about their father's or my pre-existence before they came along, they get this confused, disbelieving look on their faces as if I'm making up a story. When they examine pictures from our former military life, it's difficult for them to grasp us both as former military soldiers and as their parents. It sets up that cognitive dissonance thing I've spoken about already. For individuals who think very concretely like small children, something that is outside of their own past experience is almost impossible to grasp. As a child, I loved to hear the stories from my parents' pasts, as they seemed like movies that I would watch in my mind.

"Mama, tell me the stories of the olden days," I would say. "You know, the ones when you were a little girl," I would beg. If she was in a good mood that day, my mother would tell me the story of the escaped convict who hid out in a hole in their backyard and stole a chicken from her mother's chicken roost. Or she might tell me the story of "Porky." Porky was my mother's pet pig that my grandmother killed for dinner one night. None of the kids could eat what was on their plates that night, for thinking about their treasured friend lying before them.

I knew better than to ask my dad to tell me about his childhood. He didn't have time, or I was in the way. What I learned about his early years came from his mother, my Grandma Davis. Grandma used to love to tell me about the "olden days," especially the stories of her childhood. But I was always pestering her to get off her own childhood and tell me the stories about her own children, like my father, my aunt, and my uncles, people I knew personally.

It was from my grandmother that I learned how much my father liked homemade biscuits. In fact, though he was the namesake of my Granddaddy Davis and the "hero child" of the family, my father was known throughout my extended family as a pushover for biscuits. I can remember a meal was not a meal unless my mother made biscuits and he could eat three quarters of the pan by himself! If any were left, we would hide the peanut butter jar in the towel drawer after supper so he couldn't find it and finish off the pan!

My grandmother assured us that my father's love of biscuits was because he was weaned too soon. His brother, my Uncle Burt, came along inside of two years after my father's birth. This new baby interrupted the flow of things, so to speak, and usurped my father's exclusive claim to my grandmother's chest. Because of this premature weaning, my father developed what was known as "rickets" back then, but similar to colic today. He was undernourished, so I think my grandmother sought to compensate by filling him up with homemade biscuits.

Eventually, he grew beyond these consequences to become the only one of six children to graduate from high school. He served two years in the Navy and went to trade school in Chicago to become a mechanic.

He met my mother when she was fifteen and he was twenty-eight. He dated her for almost five years before they married. May-December marriages like theirs were quite common then. In fact, his father was fifteen years older than my grandmother, having married her when she was barely fourteen years old. And I have kept the tradition going by marrying a man sixteen years older than me. I think it must be genetic!

My father grew up during the deep depression and two world wars. He was in the Navy during the bombing of Pearl Harbor. He witnessed and experienced events that I have no experience of at all. And in his own way, he rose above his early circumstances. He stood out as the son, though third in line of his siblings, who turned out to be the most occupationally and financially stable. Still, he paid a high price to escape those early years. He died twenty-eight years ago, barely sixty-one years old, the second of the original six to die, bearing the consequences of one of his coping mechanisms, smoking. While lung cancer physically killed him, I believe he died in many ways long before that physical finality. His rigid, shame-based identity could not handle his only daughter marrying someone of a different race and color. He and my mother refused to attend our wedding or acknowledge our marriage. Sadly, he died steadfastly refusing to know the "son" he had always wanted.

As I compare the prism of my life alongside my father's and acknowledge the mistakes I've made and the amount of effort that has been required to grow and change, God's grace changes my heart toward my Daddy. Rather than being resentful of his narrow-mindedness, I have grown to feel sadness, understanding, and tolerance. I find it becomes harder to sit in judgment of others when you know you've faced similar circumstances and failed. My father and I both struggled with shame issues over the course of our lives, sometimes rising above them and sometimes falling victim.

My father was blind to the spiritual dimensions of his life until the very end, refusing to allow any discussion of life after death issues before He died. His adamant refusal, however, reawakened my search for God, and thirteen months after his death, my search ended with accepting Jesus as my Lord and Savior in a small Protestant chapel a world away in Germany. While he was afraid to look at the bigger spiritual dimension of life, his refusal set me up to spend the rest of eternity with my heavenly Father. What an irony!

In so many ways, my father was afraid of life and himself. He coped by smoking two to four packs of cigarettes a day, working day and night, and watching television. He didn't know how to have relationships. Even his idea of courtship with my mother was to park outside a bar, bring a Pepsi out to the car for her, and proceed to stay in the bar drinking for two to three hours. To his credit, he quit drinking cold turkey when he found out I was on the way, but he never stopped using things to help him cope with his own sense of shame about who he was.

All of this information has filtered into the hopper as I've strained to get a picture of life from my father's perspective. If I had to walk a mile in his shoes, what would I see and how would I view the landscape of his life through his eyes? All the indications he gave me while I was with him indicated an existence that was consistently performed everyday out of duty and responsibility. If you did what you were supposed to, rewards came in the form of monetary compensation. Working on a machine such as a car engine was intrinsically rewarding in and of itself. The satisfaction of having something he could accomplish and figure out seemed to bring satisfaction into an otherwise duty-bound existence. Other than football on TV, the rest of life was not too exciting for him. He believed that the value of life rested in day-in-and-day-out accountability and financial security.

Other family members used and relied on his financial stability. When they were short one month, they knew they could count on "Uncle Johnny" to have it. Financially speaking, he was the favorite in the family—the one everyone turned to when they needed something. Relationally speaking, however, my grandmother's favorite was her youngest son, my Uncle Skeet. He was the first of the brood to die early from a massive heart attack at age 46.

Try as he might in his lifelong quest to get his mother's attention and approval, the closest my dad came to getting attention from her was when she would approach him with an electric bill she couldn't pay or a need for a new stove or washer. I don't know if he ever heard that he was valued as a person or as a son or heard the words, "I love you." Perhaps my grandparents were just a product of the war era and my dad was just a commodity to them. Years later, with a daughter to bless, how could my father give me what he didn't know himself—valuing, affection, direction? He couldn't give me what he'd never received.

Contemplating the prism of my dad's perspective brought me up short as I realized just how little I really knew him. Unlike my brilliant champagne glasses, my father's personal perspective was a gray mystery to me. I was not able to look from the inside of him to the outside to see the world as he saw it. I find that it often becomes too easy to dismiss our fathers' lives because they never shared them with us. Perhaps if they had shared, we wouldn't be forced to stretch way past our own comfort zones to consider the life and perspective of someone we missed getting to know.

Seeing the world from someone's perspective other than our own is a confounding mystery, isn't it? In fact, it's one of the things I intend to talk to my heavenly Father about when I get to heaven. Understanding why people think and act the way they do without being able to live inside their head is impossible.

The best tool we have for placing ourselves in another person's shoes is empathy. Empathy is the ability to recreate another person's perspective and see the world the way they do. It is an invaluable communication and counseling tool and is equally effective in bridging the impasses in family relationships when we don't have personal history with them. There's just one little catch. In order to be able to employ the tool of empathy, you have to be willing to hold your own subjective views in tension as you attempt to look at a situation from different angles. This is difficult for many who haven't matured emotionally to the point of not having always to see things only from their own view. Indeed, our own subjectivity often limits us in being able to explore situations from numerous perspectives and achieve the best grasp of reality.

Just as the glass prisms of my champagne glasses reflect light in varying perspectives, each human life is also a glass prism with numerous vantage points. You and your dad share some degree of personal history. Chances are, however, that both of you see the same situations from slightly different angles based on any number of factors. The contributing factors don't matter as much as you each being able to recognize the equal validity of each other's perspective. To help you contemplate your history together, consider the following key points:

Empathy Completes Perspective Better Than Sympathy

When you feel sympathetic toward someone, you have compassion and/or pity for them or their predicament, but it doesn't require that you to try on the problem yourself to see how it feels. In other words, you can extend emotional support without feeling anything personally. However, to extend empathy toward someone requires that you view the situation from their point of view and feel how you imagine they would feel. While this requires much more personal emotional investment, it can provide much needed identification and illumination on insurmountable differences.

"And" Can Link Perspectives While "Buts" Separate

Using *and* rather than *but* to link perspectives with your dad will connect you both into a complementary view of your shared history. Rather than your view canceling out your dad's or vice versa, each of your perspectives will more completely illuminate the total picture. As an example, you could say, "I understand how your father criticized you, Dad, and I want you to know how your criticism hurt me too," instead of "Your dad may have been critical of you, but you turned your criticism on me." The first approach uses all-inclusive language that unites and invites a working alliance with your father rather than defensiveness, justification, and separation.

I've experienced the sting of exclusion and rejection before. Did my dad get those feelings from his family, who perhaps saw him only as a source of income? Since I've felt shame, guilt, and inadequacy before, perhaps my dad and I aren't as polarized in our perspectives as I might have thought. Standing for even a moment in his shoes, contemplating how ill prepared I was to be a parent, I catch a glimpse of a shared experience of insecurity and inadequacy.

Does knowing how he felt somehow excuse his actions toward me in God's eyes? Not anymore than God excuses my actions. God's Word promises that we will be judged by the same yardstick as we judge others. If my whining and excuses aren't bought by my heavenly Father when I don't measure up, I doubt the possibility that my dad's justifications were any more excusable. Instead, our loving heavenly Father extends grace to us if we will receive it. Abounding grace that enhances the meager offerings of need-meeting that I offer to my own children. Miraculous grace that causes heroes to grow from zeroes and sufficient grace that can turn lives birthed in the pain of inadequate fathering totally around.

The Pillow Method

Now I want to turn to a very helpful tool that can enable you to view your situation from your dad's point of view. It's called the Pillow Method, simply because you can fit all five perspectives on the face of a pillow.[1] After the following explanation, you will find a picture of how the Pillow Method actually looks on paper.

POSITION ONE: "I'm right, you're wrong." This should be a most familiar position to many of us. Sadly, it may be the only perspective we ever assume in any discussion. "I'm right, you're wrong" is the black/white, all or none thinking that young children can often lock themselves into before they have the mental ability to take another person's perspective. (We discussed this concept of egocentrism in chapter 2.) This very narrow view of reality shuts out much-needed explanations, but keeps individuals safe at the center of their own little world.

POSITION TWO: "I'm wrong, you're right." This position is largely underused by most of us. It's so difficult to admit our mistakes and accept that someone else may have a better way. Many people steer clear of this perspective entirely, believing that if they entertain it in the slightest, they will have to forfeit their own view entirely. Not so! Remember, empathy allows us to try on our dad's perspective to see how it looks and feels—not give up our own perspective. If you looked at your situation from your dad's shoes as a post-war dad, unloved, or missing a dad himself, how does the lay of the land look through his glasses?

POSITION THREE: "We're both right, we're both wrong."

If you can make the transition from Position One to Position Two, you're home free because the rest is a piece of cake! In Position Three, we use that all-inclusive *and* to connect our perspective with our dad's, even though they may seem miles apart.

"Dad, you're right about the need to discipline children, and I needed your affection as well as your discipline."

"I'm not sure either one of us had a clue how to be a parent when we first started out. At least we've got that in common."

POSITION FOUR: The relationship is more important than the issue. Relationships that can go the distance are in the minority. Often times relatives look back and realize they may have sacrificed a lifetime of relationship for a less than significant argument. It's sad when the fight to win individual battles in relationships supersedes the importance of winning the war for that relationship. Sometimes we have to ask ourselves, "Is this issue (fill in the blank) more important than having a relationship?" When we hold our subjective perspective more loosely and feel secure enough to examine others' perspectives, we discover that we do not hold an absolute corner on truth. In fact, we may even find that we can forgive some issues without compromising ourselves or destroying relationships. When we can reach a point where we can talk through issues, choosing to release some and integrating our perspective with our dad on others, we may find a relationship worth salvaging.

POSITION FIVE: Truth in all four perspectives.

Here we come upon the big picture. None of us has absolute truth. Each of us has a slice. If we put our perspectives together, seeing the pros and cons, and still agree that having a healthy relationship is the most important priority, we have developed as much cognitive complexity as needed. Perspective-taking builds empathy and identification with each other. Learning to identify is a way to draw close to your parent when all else may fail. Over a period of time, practicing empathy with our dads kneads grace into our hearts. A sense of elasticity grows, which helps us grow beyond the bondage of our wounds to embrace others, like our fathers, who are as needy as we are, if not more so.

	Position One	
	I'm Right, You're Wrong	
Position Two	*Position Five*	*Position Four*
I'm Wrong, You're Right	Truth in All Four Perspectives	Relationship is More Important
	Position Three	
	Both Right, Both Wrong	

ONE FINAL WORD OF ENCOURAGEMENT

I cannot over stress the importance of going through the above empathy exercise to connect your perspective and your dad's in a healthy way. Many father-wound class participants tell me this was a critical piece of their healing, and for others it becomes a major obstacle they must clear before healing is complete.

Father Prisms

Though you may be afraid at first to even peek at your dad's point of view, it will not harm you to do so. Many individuals believe initially that to see things from their dad's perspective means they must relinquish their own perspective, thereby negating their dad's responsibility and guilt for wounding them. This couldn't be further from the truth. Holding onto just your side of the truth is only half of the total picture. Standing for a moment in your dad's shoes will not compromise your control. However, I will say it may change you … most likely for the better! Gazing at your father prism will build empathy as you find yourself often understanding how and why he saw his life as he did. When you behold how you could have ended up (perhaps just like him), but didn't, you may find yourself on your knees to your Father in heaven in thankfulness and gratitude. God our heavenly Father desires to save all of us from the sins of the fathers, if we will but ask.

> I, the Lord your God, am a jealous God, punishing the children for the sins of the fathers to the third and fourth generation of those who hate me, but showing love to a thousand generations of those who love me and keep my commandments.
> —Exodus 20:5

CHAPTER SEVEN

Group Study Questions

1. Do you see your perspective of life with your dad as being valid?

2. What is your perspective of what happened between you and your dad?

3. What do you think your dad's perspective is of you and his relationship with you?

4. Can you hold these differing perspectives in tension with each other using the word "and" rather than "but"? Try and formulate a few statements that link your perspectives.

5. Is it difficult for you to look at your own perspective without negating your dad's, or vice versa?

6. What do you know of your dad's life before you came along? How does this affect the way he fathered you?

CHAPTER SEVEN

Homework Questions

1. Please imagine for a moment that you are your father's mother or father, i.e. your grandmother or grandfather. What words of encouragement could your grandmother or grandfather have spoken to your father that may have made a difference in his life? As the "wise" parent of your father, what could have been given to him that he, in turn did not give to you? After you have considered this, write a letter to your dad, from either of his parents, that offers him what he needed and didn't get.

2. What feelings and thoughts came up for you as you wrote the letter in Question 1?

3. Let's pretend you go to sleep tonight and your father speaks to you from a miracle dream. In that dream your dad has acquired some wisdom and speaks to you what you have always needed to hear from him. What does he say to you? Record what you believe the Holy Spirit is saying to you through this exercise.

4. After you have done exercise 3 above, picture yourself speaking on behalf of the child you once were. Tell your father what you need from him now, or how you wish the relationship between the two of you to be. Allow yourself to speak truthful, healing words to your father so that you will be released from the power your child's perspective is holding over you.

Forgiveness Is a Choice

Philip Yancey, in his book *What's So Amazing About Grace,* tells story after story of political and historical atrocities that have choked our world. In one such story, he tells of a meeting in 1991 between Soviet leaders and a delegation of Christians, including Yancey, which took place in the offices of the KGB (the intelligence arm of the Soviet Union). Political unrest reigned at this time. Boris Yeltsin was consolidating power and support day by day as he tried to wrestle the Soviet Union from Mikhail Gorbachev. In light of this most recent unrest, the Soviet leadership had requested the meeting with Christian leaders to help restore some sense of morality in their country. As Yancey tells it, the Christian leaders braced themselves for a somewhat cooler reception that night at the KGB headquarters than the previous warm receptions they had received from Soviet government officials. Imagine their surprise, however, when the Vice-Chairman of the KGB, General Nikilai Stolyarov, said the following:

> "Meeting with you here tonight," General Stolyarov began, "is a plot twist that could not have been conceived by the wildest fiction writer." He had that right. Then he startled us by saying, "We here in the USSR realize that too often we've been negligent in accepting those of the Christian faith. But political questions cannot

be decided until there is sincere repentance, a return to faith by the people. That is the cross I must bear. In the study of scientific atheism, there was the idea that religion divides peoples. Now we see the opposite: love for God can only unite."[1]

Yancey paints a picture of startled surprise in the Christian delegation. Repentance? Where had the KGB learned to use a word like repentance? Yancey goes on to say that the General was dared to be challenged by an individual from the Christian delegation who questioned the sincerity of the General's remarks with the reminder that many of those present in the visiting Christian delegation had lost family members in the Russian prison. As Yancey proceeds, the KGB general replies, "I have spoken of repentance. This is an essential step. There can be no perestroika apart from repentance. The time has come to repent of that past. We have broken the Ten Commandments, and for this we pay today."[2]

Immediately upon the KGB general's acknowledgement of ownership, Alex Leonovich, stood to speak. A member of the Christian delegation and a native of Byelorussia who managed to escape during Stalin's reign, eventually emigrating to the US where he had been a radio broadcaster sending Christian programs (often jammed) back to the Soviet Union. First he reminded the general that members of his personal family had suffered under the terror of the KGB. He further reminded him that he himself was forced to leave his motherland and was shipped to a labor camp in Siberia. He concluded by saying, "General, you say that you repent. Christ taught us how to respond. On behalf of my family and on behalf of my uncle who died in the Gulag, I forgive you." And then this big Russian Christian reached over and gave the KGB vice-chair a huge Russian bear hug."[3]

Many were speechless at this unexpected turn of events. Some even doubted the sincerity of the KGB leadership, believing it all to be an act. However as Yancey notes, the Soviet leadership continues to be challenged and their motives questioned.

As Americans, we know from experience not to trust the Soviet Union. However, more than our distrust, Russians do not trust one another or their government either, because many of them have personally lived through the heinous atrocities inflicted on them by their government. Yancey realistically reminds us that the past must be remembered before it can be overcome.

History must be overcome, however slowly, if repentance is to be proven the genuine article. Here in the U.S., we are growing ever so slowly but surely beyond our own national atrocities and racial tensions. Though a slow work to be sure, we keep moving as a nation toward complete ownership of the racial inequities and crimes against our fellow man. While pockets of racial unrest still remain, and spotty factions of racism still rise up here and there, overall, we as a nation are moving past our wrongs. In order to do that, we have had to look at our past mistakes, own them, and grow past them.

Absolute, pure forgiveness can be granted only when repentance is extended. For repentance to be sincere, it must be willing to look at the past. Too often I hear the phrase, "You need to forgive and forget." Or what about, "You need to forget and move on." And while there's a grain of truth in both of these exhortations, the reality is that many of us struggle with remembering and wonder if we've really forgiven when we can still remember the wrongs done to us. The question begs to be asked whether true forgiveness must involve forgetting or remembering.

Now most of us know already that God's example of forgiveness is to remove our sins as far as the east is from the west (Ps. 103:12), and He remembers our sins no more (Is. 43:25). He actually invites us to review our past with Him in Isaiah 43:26, but as far as He is concerned, once we have acknowledged the sin, He puts it behind us. Are we able to do that? Should we do that? We question and we parse words as we struggle in our finiteness to analyze just what God requires of us in the area of forgiveness.

The disciples were no strangers to trying to understand forgiveness, either. Matthew 18:21 tells of their questioning of Jesus, "Lord how many times shall I forgive my brother when he sins against me? Up to seven times?" Jesus answered, "I tell you the truth, not seven times but seventy-seven times" (Matt. 18:22). As He often did during His short ministry on earth, Jesus used this particular occasion to illustrate His point with a story:

Therefore the kingdom of heaven is like a king who wanted to settle accounts with his servants. As he began the settlement, a man who owed him ten thousand talents was brought to him. Since he was not able to pay, the master ordered that he and his wife and his children and all that he had be sold to repay the debt. The servant fell on his knees before him. "Be patient with me," he begged, "and I will pay back everything." The servant's master took pity on him, canceled the debt and let him go. But when that servant went out, he found one of his fellow servants who owed him a hundred denarii. He grabbed him and began to choke him. "Pay back what you owe me!" he demanded. His fellow servant fell to his knees and begged him, "Be patient with me, and I will pay you back." But he refused. Instead, he went off and had the man thrown into prison until he could pay the debt. When the other servants saw what had happened, they were greatly distressed and went and told their master everything that had happened. Then the master called the servant in. "You wicked servant," he said, "I canceled all that debt of yours because you begged me to. Shouldn't you have had mercy on your fellow servant just as I had on you?" In anger his master turned him over to the jailers to be tortured, until he should pay back all he owed. This is how my heavenly Father will treat each of you unless you forgive your brother from your heart.

—Matt. 18:23-35

Just what was Jesus getting at? Is he saying that we are to forgive and forget? Is He saying we are to have boundless forgiveness?

You know, repeated rereading of this passage doesn't yield any words suggesting that forgiveness equals forgetting. What Jesus does do is rebuke behavior that springs from a heart that keeps accounts. Accountability is a form of the word *accounts*. I think what Jesus is suggesting is that we cannot hold each other "accountable" to our ledger of wrongs. Perhaps He is saying we are to release those who have accounts with us just as He (our master) has released us.

During the last several weeks, we have been doing a lot of remembering haven't we? You have been looking at your relationship with your earthly dad far more honestly than you ever have before. Not only have you come upon more of his faults than you ever thought possible, but you have also witnessed pockets of pain in your heart that you didn't know were there before. God knew. He knows us better than we know ourselves, doesn't He? Scripture says, "Man looks on the outward appearance, but the Lord looks at the heart" (1 Sam. 16:7).

I believe the first step in the process of forgiveness is honesty—honesty with ourselves and before our God. Hopefully, by now all of your secrets have come out about the dad of your past and been exposed to God-filtered air. You have taken a good, hard look at what you missed out on, and have allowed yourself some time to grieve those losses. You have written letters, outlined your father's crimes against you, and looked at your responses to his faults. As we finish up this part of the process, it's good to acknowledge that we're all still alive! Looking at those secrets and turning over those rocks truly did not kill us, like many may have thought. Remembering has brought some benefit to all of us as our perspectives have changed. Indeed, without remembering and examining the parenting mistakes of our past, many of us would unintentionally perpetuate them on our children and grandchildren. Remembering is necessary. Without it, we can stay locked in invisible bondage to our past.

FORGIVENESS FOR YOURSELF

South Africa's healing from the racial atrocities of apartheid offers us valuable wisdom about the essentials of the forgiveness process. As parts of that continent worked their way through to individual and national healing, it became apparent that one of the requirements of forgiveness included individuals forgiving for themselves, not having someone act on their behalf. Secondly, there must be full disclosure for forgiveness and healing to take place. And finally forgiveness must be requested by the offending party before it can be granted. As Phil Yancey states, "South Africans are remembering their past in order to forget it."[4]

We are struck with a very important truth here. True forgiveness requires remembering. We must be informed about what we are forgiving, as well as confessing ownership of the crimes we've inflicted. However, forgiveness must also release accountability; at least to us.

While there has been great benefit in coming to grips with our personal pain, ventilating it, and grieving our wounds, there comes a point when you have to ask yourself, "What do I get from holding onto these grievances? I've talked about them. My friends know them. God knew them before I did. Holding on to them will not increase my father's accountability to me or God. Holding on to them does not ensure that my father will pay in the way I see fit." Indeed, Rom. 12:19 says, "Do not take revenge, my friends, but leave room for God's wrath, for it is written, 'It is mine to avenge; I will repay,' says the Lord. Now I ask you, who presents a more threatening picture, you or the Living God?" What's that you say? What if God forgives your dad instead of making him pay? What if He does? Can He do that? Sure He can. He's God. He's our Creator, He can do anything He wants. Who is your father more accountable to, you or God? After all, you are God's work, His kid, created in His image. Who better to avenge you?

Of course, we could all be Jonahs here. Remember Jonah. He was disobedient to God's direction because he was afraid God would forgive Nineveh if he preached there and they repented. Jonah didn't want forgiveness for Nineveh. He wanted revenge. And he had a spiritual conflict with God because God chose to be God instead of jumping to do Jonah's bidding. So Jonah pouted under a God-provided weed until he was able to accept who was in charge of him and Nineveh. Sometimes by holding onto our grievances, we create our own bondage and pain. At some point, we have to accept and acknowledge who's in charge.

God, our heavenly Father, is in charge of His kids, and being the good parent He is, He doesn't allow us or anyone else to make His decisions for Him. Nobody tells Him how to raise His kids. They are accountable to Him and Him alone.

Forgiveness is remembering and releasing. However, it doesn't change the consequences. We can release our fathers from their debt to us, but it doesn't have to change safe boundaries that we may have to set around our relationship. We may forgive and release a father from our accountability, but the restrictions and consequences live on so there may not be future offenses. Child abusers are forgiven, but they still must not be around children. And we have laws now against discrimination and racism to safeguard us from past abuses in history repeating themselves. These consequences are part of the loving discipline of forgiveness. Restrictions and consequences set up safe arenas so that forgiveness can prevail.

WITH GOD, ALL THINGS ARE POSSIBLE

At times forgiveness and reconciliation can seem impossible. Humanly speaking, it is next to impossible to let go. The process of release requires supernatural help from God and it often doesn't happen overnight. It is a process that can happen in phases.

Forgiveness is first and foremost an intellectual decision to release the person from the debt they owe us. Webster's New World Dictionary gives this definition of the word forgiveness: "to give up resentment against or the desire to punish." The first step toward forgiveness is honesty with God and ourselves. Have we remembered our grievances and attached emotions to our losses? Have we given full acknowledgment to those offenses which require forgiveness?

Once we have grieved sufficiently, we can make the intellectual decision to release the person to the accountability of God, their Creator and Father, and ours. This release requires us to let go of our pain (maybe in the form of our own defenses, like anger) for our own good. If your wound has drained adequately, forgiveness can move beyond a choice of the intellect to an experience of the heart, where you emotionally let go of the pain attached to that grievance. Holding onto the pain in the hope it will receive future attention serves no earthly good and keeps us chained to that grievance.

When we choose to forgive our fathers, we are not saying what they did was right or that they were not responsible for their offenses. Rather, we are saying, "My father is no longer answerable or responsible to me. I choose this day to give up his debt to me."

Choosing to forgive a grievance doesn't require the confession and repentance of the guilty party. Exercising the choice to forgive unhooks us from the clutches of their sin and reattaches them to God's accountability. From the cross, Jesus pronounced his own counter-sentence, striking an eternal blow against unforgiveness because He forgave those who had not even repented when He said,

"Father, forgive them for they do not know what they are doing." Choosing to forgive simply requires our obedience to a Father who has already forgiven us far more and asks us to extend the same grace to others.

If you have grieved the loss of your dad and practice giving up making him accountable to you, you will realize in several weeks that it doesn't seem as overwhelming as it once did. You will find yourself analyzing your responses and choosing one that best represents you, rather than impulsively reacting to the dad of your past.

As you consider this whole topic of forgiveness and whether now is the time for you to make that choice in your healing process, pull out the list of grievances you wrote out some chapters back. Look at the items you placed on this list and determine whether there are any you feel differently about now than when you originally wrote the list. Has your attitude shifted in any way on these issues? Is there anything you need to accept responsibility for now that you see was yours? Are there others who contributed to the problem, rather than laying all the blame on your father? You may find that you can forgive your father for only a few of your grievances at this point; other items on your list may still seem unpardonable. Whatever the case, how would you complete this sentence at this point in time: I can now choose to forgive my father for _____.

At this time, it's also good to write out a testimony of how this Father-healing process is changing your heart. It's even better if you can share pieces of that testimony with a small group of friends. Also if you are a creative person or have ideas concerning setting up memorials to the hard work you have done or to honor the honorable parts of your father, please use your ideas to mark this milestone in your growth. This is an important time of making choices about what to leave behind as we move toward future restoration.

CHAPTER EIGHT

Group Study Questions

1. Discuss your grievance list from Session 6. Are there some items on the list that you are willing to forgive your dad for now?

2. Which items on your list are you willing to give up to God for His collection of debt against you?

3. On a scale of 1 to 10, how honest have you been before God about those things that have hurt you from the past with your dad? Have you exposed all your known hurts to God-filtered air?

4. Discuss Romans 12:19 with your group. How difficult is it for you to submit your dad to God for divine retribution?

5. What are your experiences with forgiveness up to this point? Has it come miraculously for you, or is it a process?

CHAPTER EIGHT

Homework Questions

1. Spend some time this week with the Lord concerning your understanding of forgiveness with your dad. If you're unsure, ask God what He would have you relinquish to Him.

2. At this point, are you feeling any sense of release? If so, try to express to your small group what you believe you are releasing to your heavenly Father.

3. Write out a two-page testimony of what changes have taken place in your heart so far concerning your perspective of your father.

4. Now that you are no longer under your father's hold over you, is there anything positive that he gave to you? Don't be concerned if you can't think of anything at this point. If there is an item worthy of honor, think about how you could honor that part of your dad. Try filling in the following sentence, "I honor my father, _____, for _____.

4. Begin thinking of possibilities for making a "memorial" to the healing that you have done so far. Is there something you could make, write, or put together that would serve as a reminder to you that this part of your healing is complete?

Say Hello to Your Inner Child!

H as somebody ever said to you, "Why don't you just get over it?!" Or what about this one: "Grow up!" Have you ever secretly wished that you could just blink your eyes and all the pain would go away? Unfortunately, "getting over it" isn't always easy, is it? Sometimes, it seems the harder we work, the more we spin our wheels. In order to get out of this rut, it's necessary to gain some perspective on applying Paul's counsel in 1 Corinthians 13:11: "When I was a child, I talked like a child, I thought like a child, I reasoned like a child. When I became a man, I put childish ways behind me."

You may be familiar with the context of this verse. Paul is writing to the Corinthians about some of their abuses within the early church. In particular, in chapter 13 he has just admonished them about the lack of love they show toward one another. He ends his definition of love with this verse that encourages them to move beyond their childish practices and perceptions of love to more mature thinking and behavior. But just as the Corinthians struggled with growing into maturity, we Christians today, even in the new millenium, still struggle with overcoming childhood thoughts, perceptions, and behaviors as we seek to pursue Christ's perfect work in our lives.

Dr. Hugh Missildine, a child psychiatrist, puts it this way in his landmark book of 1963, *Your Inner Child of the Past:*

The child you once were continues to survive inside your adult shell. "Thrive" would perhaps be a better word than "survive," for often this "inner child of the past" is a sprawling, bawling, brawling character—racing pell-mell into activities he/she likes, dawdling, cheating, lying to get out of things they don't like, upsetting and wrecking others' lives. Or perhaps this child is the fearful, timid, tearful, shrinking part of your personality. Whether we like it or not, we are simultaneously the child we once were, who lives in the emotional atmosphere of the past and often interferes in the present, and an adult who tries to forget the past and live wholly in the present. The child you once were can balk or frustrate your adult satisfactions, embarrass or harass you, make you sick—or enrich your life.[1]

As Christians, hopefully our goal is to grow up, becoming full-fledged, mature adults in Christ. However, most of us fail at times, and the "inner child" within us takes over and runs the show! Many well-meaning Christians think the fastest road to spiritual and emotional maturity is to forget about this inner child altogether. They think and say, "If I don't acknowledge this part of myself, it doesn't exist." WRONG! Most of us find out the hard way that if we want a recipe for disaster in our lives, just try ignoring our inner child. They will embarrass us every time! All you have to do is go through one situation where you said the wrong thing at the wrong time, or lost control of your feelings, or yelled at your kids to know that little person you once were, never dies.

However, just because the inner child still exists in all of us, we aren't necessarily doomed to repeat all of our same old mistakes or find them taking over and running our lives. If we let the inner child rule the roost, he/she will! However, when our inner child and our adult selves work in cooperation and unity, we can accomplish God's will for our lives with less sabotage and far more of the peace Paul talked about in Phil. 4:6-7. How many of you would like more peace with yourself?

If you do desire internal peace, then say "Hello" to your inner child! It is the impulsive, sensitive, and most creative part of you. Paradoxically, it is you at your most inspired moments and also in the moments you wish you could forget.

Say Hello To Your Inner Child!

In order to foster their cooperation, our inner child must feel heard. To accomplish that, we must go back and pick up on the feelings that go with our childish perspective without stepping all over them in the process. Though it sounds mysterious, this doesn't have to be a tedious process. Actually, it can be rather fun getting to know the little child that exists inside. By coming to know this part of yourself, you can paradoxically build trust in yourself to act maturely in situations instead of self-indulgently acting out. Building cooperation between the adult you and the child you once were involves establishing a trust alliance between you. The child part desperately wants to know that you (the adult) will listen to that part of yourself and take their needs into consideration instead of tuning them out. The adult part begins to see that the child part will cooperate if listened to and self-sabotage decreases. The internal dialogue can go something like this:

ADULT: "What am I hungry for this morning?

INNER CHILD: "Let's have chocolate cake and Rocky Road ice cream!"

ADULT: "It's breakfast. We can't have chocolate cake and ice cream!"

INNER CHILD: "Why?"

ADULT: "We just can't. We have to set an example for the kids."

INNER CHILD: "Why?"

ADULT: "Well, because, that's why."

INNER CHILD: "Why?"

ADULT: "OK, I know we like cake and ice cream. But the kids need cereal or hot food to get them ready to learn in school."

INNER CHILD: "But I want ice cream...now!"

ADULT: "How about this? We eat cereal with the kids now and later before we pick them up for school, we have a single scoop of Rocky Road from Baskin Robbins. Can you live with that?

INNER CHILD: "OK, but only if you promise.

ADULT: "I promise."

Or consider this scenario:

ADULT: "Boy, that sure was a rough meeting tonight. I wish we all agreed more."

INNER CHILD: "Yeah, that Charmaine Tibbs, I hate her for what she said. I just want to punch her lights out!"

ADULT: "Now, you know we can't do that. It wouldn't be Christian."

INNER CHILD: "Who cares? I just want to get her to shut up!"

ADULT: "I guess I really was hurt by what Charmaine said, huh."

INNER CHILD: "Yeah, you need to get her back!"

ADULT: "Yeah, it might feel good to hurt her the way she hurt me."

INNER CHILD: "Yeah, then we can punch her!"

ADULT: "Well, I don't know...I am a Bible Study Leader. That might not look too good."

INNER CHILD: "Who cares! You'll feel better if you get her!"

ADULT: "I don't know about that. I may feel worse. How about, we ask God about it. After all, He loves us whether Charmaine does or not."

INNER CHILD: "Well, OK, but He's usually a party pooper. We never get to punch anybody when He comes into the picture."

ADULT: Well, yeah. But He also says, "Vengeance is mine. I will repay. Who's bigger—us or God?"

INNER CHILD: "God. OK, but if He says we can punch her, let me do it, OK?"

Hopefully, I'm not too out of touch with where real people live in their internal world. The point I'm trying to make is this: Your inner child can be reasoned with, if you take the time to listen to your own unspoken and unmet needs. The Holy Spirit can be very faithful in revealing our selves to us if we will but listen internally.

The problem for many of us is that we're not tuned in to what those childhood needs are that didn't get met. What did you need as a child? We've already looked at this issue from one angle back in chapter 4. Then I asked you to list what you didn't get from your dad that you needed. Look back at that list right now and see if you remember why those needs were so important. That list reflects what your inner child needed and didn't receive in sufficiency.

Is your list purely subjective based on your inner child's wants, or is there some objective reality to what's on it? Which items would show up on every kid's need list? We've spent most of our time up to this point looking at what was dysfunctional about the fathering we received. I want to focus us right now on looking at this issue more directly. Just what do children need to grow to be healthy adults? Compare your list to the points that follow.

Abraham Maslow, a grandfather of psychology, says that the needs of human beings can be placed in a hierarchy ranging from physical needs all the way to what he refers to as self-actualization needs.[2]

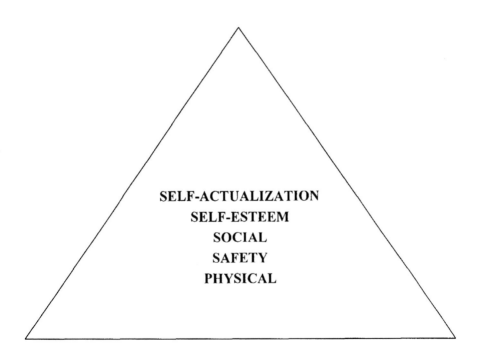

SELF-ACTUALIZATION
SELF-ESTEEM
SOCIAL
SAFETY
PHYSICAL

PHYSICAL NEEDS: First of all, children have physical needs that have to be satisfied by parents. They are born into the world in a dependent state. They are dependent on parents for feeding them, changing them, making sure they have water or milk to drink, and clean air to breathe. These are the most basic physical needs of a human being and the place where we all start.

Fathers are especially important in providing an environment that meets these physical needs in an orderly way. Children who grow up in neglectful circumstances, not having their physical needs attended to, receive the unspoken message, "You don't exist. You don't count. You are not a real person." Indeed, some experts are only now realizing and identifying that children who grow up in physical deprivation grow up with an inadequate sense of self, and they are unable to adequately form relationships with others. This ultimately results in a lack of conscience development and a poor ability to identify and empathize with others. These individuals cannot feel for another person, because they can't even feel for themselves.

SAFETY NEEDS: Fathers are also responsible for protecting their children and keeping them safe from outside influences and the world. A laissez-faire, permissive dad will expose his child to hidden dangers. A father teaches his child that he/she is valuable and worth keeping safe. A dad who provides safety and protection keeps a child's anxiety at bay. A young child shouldn't have to worry that his house might burn down or that his parent will wreck the car and hurt him. A good father teaches his child through his protective behaviors that his child matters to him.

SOCIAL/EMOTIONAL NEEDS: Children have social and emotional needs that fathers are responsible for facilitating. Understanding emotional needs is a prerequisite for building healthy relationships in the future. Emotional needs that are left unfulfilled do not simply evaporate into thin air! We just carry them into adulthood and unintentionally transfer them onto others. Even promising ourselves that we will never be like our parents can often set us up for the exact opposite unhealthy option! That's why it is so important to understand emotional needs and their impact, even in healthy families. Children learn how to relate and get along with others through their dad's introduction to the outside world beyond mom.

Remembering emotional needs in an ABC format is helpful in giving us a clue about how and why we seek the relationships we do.[3] There are four A's, one B, and one C:

Affection: This need is met by both physical, verbal, and non-verbal expressions of love, caring, and emotional commitment. Physical touch, such as hugging or gentle squeezing, loving words, facial expressions that use smiles and plenty of eye contact all communicate to others that we care about them.

Acceptance: All of us need to know that our unique blend of characteristics, personality traits, talents, gifts, and abilities are welcomed and encouraged by others. When the need for acceptance is met, a child feels secure in being who she is.

Being accepted for who we actually are keeps us from pretending to be what we perceive others want us to be, such as people pleasing.

Approval: When this need is met adequately, a child feels more than just accepted. He/she sees their personal uniqueness as being good and special in the eyes of others. Children who feel approval know they are of value and important to others. Feeling approval from dad is a necessary stepping stone to feeling approved by our heavenly Father.

Attention: All of us have some inherent need to be noticed and attended to in connecting with others. Paying attention to someone communicates to them that they exist, they are important, and they matter to the person giving the attention. So important is this need for attention that most human beings will try and get it one way or another. If there isn't enough positive attention to satisfy, children often resort to negative attention, figuring that negative attention is better than no attention at all! Adequate attention requires time attendance by mothers and fathers. Spending time listening, sharing, and responding to children pays big dividends in the development of self-esteem.

Belonging: Making sure a child knows he belongs to his dad is very important for emotional security and building self-esteem. Kids may seem embarrassed when we claim them publicly, but inside they glow, especially if we have set a respectable role model. Almost without exception, when I hear a dad on the sidelines at a baseball game say proudly, "That's my boy!" I don't have to look too far to see a red-faced boy not working very hard to hide the biggest grin in town. We need to know to whom we belong. Belonging is so key that if a child doesn't have it set in very early, they will look for places or people to whom they can cling, so they will feel as if they belong. Children can struggle with identity issues as a natural part of human development. Knowing that, dads can clarify those natural struggle points with clear messages that define who they are and whose they are. Dads anchor their children in helping them to realize that they belong to something bigger than themselves, i.e. family and relationships. When we as parents fail to meet this important need, anxiety grows and manifests itself as individuals try to find themselves in being bonded to something/someone outside of themselves.

Competence: Human beings have a need to know they can take care of themselves. Feeling inadequate or incomplete in life's tasks stokes the fires of insecurity that can undermine the best of us. To know we have some abilities we are good at helps to offset and compensate for deficits in other areas. No individual is totally self-sustaining. We are all fallen and incomplete. That is why we need a Savior. However, knowing we have strengths and abilities can help us rise above falling victim to factors which we have no control over in life. Helping and nurturing a child's strengths and competence in areas causes self-confidence to grow and can also be a faith-builder in their personal relationship with God.

SELF-ESTEEM NEEDS: Proverbs 22:6 says, "Train a child in the way he should go, and when he is old he will not turn from it." Some translations read, "train up a child according to his bent." There are several perspectives on this verse. Some individuals believe it has to do with the spiritual training a child receives at home, some believe it has to do with a child's natural abilities, and still others believe that the "bent" of a child has to do with his personality or temperament type. I say, "all of the above."

The most important gift a dad can give a child is to look at his own child for his/her gifting and encourage them in that direction. So often a child's self-esteem suffers because parents don't look to the child they have, but to an invisible child they set up as a comparison. Or perhaps a child is viewed through the distortions of the father's sensitivity to his own shortcomings. Self-esteem grows as children receive their father's undivided time and attention. They need to be able to talk with him and sound ideas off him so they feel secure in holding their own with others. Children who miss out on these powerful moments with dad spend much of their lives trying to reassure themselves they are adequate to the task of life. Training up a child according to his/her gifting goes a long way towards developing the life competence all of us need to stay the course.

SELF-ACTUALIZATION NEEDS: Finally, a father must meet the need of his child to self-actualize by helping to launch him or her into the world. Since Dad is the connection with the outside world, children need a blessing and release by dad to go their own way in the world when it comes time. Children need to talk about their aspirations, possible directions, options, and choices long before the "lift-off" comes. When children can become the best person God intended them to be, they are ready for the world and the world had better get ready for them!

What about you? How well did your dad meet your basic needs as a human being? How needy do you still feel and act? Need some help? Take a look at your inner child. This will let you in on the neglected areas of your life. Take inventory. In the coming weeks we will help you address those deficits, so you can "grow yourself up."

Playtime!

Many of us have been adult children or children walking around in adult bodies for a long time. Some of us have never gotten a chance to be kids. Many of us do not even know how to relax or play. Take some time this week to change that. Find an activity you remember as a child, like making mud pies, playing cowboys and Indians, working with clay, coloring pictures, etc., and then do it! Yes, I did say that. Take some time out for yourself and play! You can do this, I promise. If you're doing this work in a small group, then play together as a small group. I like to use clay that I get at the craft store and ask people to fashion their favorite toy or memory from childhood. Then we bring our creations together and share our memories. It always proves to be a highlight in my father-wound classes. I hope you will take the time to let your inner child have permission to play.

DADDYLOGUES

Another source of support or tool is a "Daddylogue." Take verses of Scripture and personalize them as God speaking to you. Marie Chapian's devotional books are a personal favorite of mine, because they depict scriptural conversations between God and me that nurture me and help me to believe in myself and God's love for me. They give me food for thought as I picture what I need to hear from my loving ABBA. Here is one example of a Daddylogue that God gave to me that meets my need:

> I love you and believe in you. I stand behind you one-hundred percent. I know you are talented and gifted. You can do anything you set your mind to do. I see how determined you are. Keep faith in yourself and my desires to bless you. I support you in whatever you determine you should do. I have given you a destiny in this world. There is a place that only you can fill. Stand up for yourself. Voice your opinions and feelings with faith and courage. You are respectable and deserve to be treated respectfully. You are a loving person and want to share this love with others. I am proud to be your father, and I accept you totally as you really are.

I suggest that you record your daddylogues on tape or a personalized version of Scripture and play it as you fall asleep at night. Being able to sleep in the arms and care of a protective father fulfills some of the deepest needs many of us carry. The Holy Spirit can use God's words to minister to the deepest needs we have. Allow Him to fill you up.

CHAPTER NINE

Group Exercise

Today you will be doing a tactile exercise in your small groups with clay. After you warm the clay up so it is pliable, please create something that represents the child who lives inside you. Maybe it will be a favorite toy from childhood or a picture that is pleasing to your inner child. While you are working, talk with your group about what you needed as a child.

CHAPTER NINE

Homework Questions

1. What are some of the unmet needs you still carry from childhood that interfere with your life and/or relationships today?

2. In what areas has your view of your pain not been allowed to grow beyond the child's perspective?

3. If you could imagine a father, any father, yours, God, or an imaginary dad, saying encouraging words that could address your inner child's needs, what would this father say to you? Feel free to use extra resources to construct your Daddylogue, such as the Bible, devotional books, or your own creative writing abilities. Construct a Daddylogue and put it on an audiotape. Begin to listen to this tape at night as you fall asleep.

Reparenting Like the Father

W hich of you, if his son asks for bread, will give him a stone? Or if he asks for a fish, will give him a snake? If you, then, though you are evil, know how to give good gifts to your children, how much more will your Father in heaven give good gifts to those who ask him!" (Matt. 7:9-11).

As we've been looking at the legacy of unmet needs that you carry, are you getting a picture yet of how the fathering you received shapes up? How did your dad do when it came to meeting the physical, safety, social, or self-esteem needs we've been talking about? Did you get from him what you needed? Was it enough?

Most of us sadly realize that in many cases we didn't receive what we needed in order to grow into well-adjusted people. If you haven't grasped it already, you're now beginning to sense that humans are a needy bunch! None of us has received a sufficiency of those needs mentioned in the last chapter. I'm needy in areas that perhaps you're not, and you're needy in areas that I feel filled.

From the beginning of our journey from pain to peace through our father-wounding, we have been discovering there are no perfect fathers or parents on earth. Once we are able to accept this truth, we realize another staggering reality. We are all father-wounded! Since the fall of mankind, human beings have been separated from our heavenly Father. Only through Jesus Christ's redeeming us, do we even begin to have the potential to be healed from our innate father-woundedness. Just because you're having to work out this healing process doesn't make you flawed or a throw-away in our heavenly Father's family. You're just further along in your healing, because you at least recognize you need a Father's touch.

Many individuals, including saved, Bible-believing, Spirit-filled Christians, do not receive the Father's healing touch because they don't even know they need it. Perhaps the world around them knows they're needy and missing something, but they aren't yet ready to receive the blessing of a Father's love. I was this way for years. Blundering along, oblivious that I wore my woundedness for the world to see with every emotional over-reaction and every addictive behavior, I thought I was destined to carry my woundedness to my grave.

Because we live in a fallen world, most of us arrive in adulthood carrying baggage from the past. Sometimes through adult mistakes and/or our own denial, we can compound that baggage, making a giant outdoor trash bag full of pain from a tall kitchen bag! However, there is one who desires to be our all-sufficient protector, caretaker, and father. God desires to teach us how to see ourselves as He sees us and to love ourselves as He loves us. This is not a self-centered, worldly kind of self-focused love, but a nurturing, encouraging reaching to be our very best kind of love. The kind of love that is gentle and gracious with others because it springs from an inner well that is filled by receiving God's generosity and grace to us.

Humankind is in need of an all-sufficient Father who can first make us aware of our needs, and then supply the provisions for meeting those needs in Him. Many times, though, we can just be so consumed with our own neediness, our own sense of deprivation, that we can't see the provision. Isn't that what happened to Israel? They became so consumed with their victimization, deprivation, and perceived abandonment by God that they whined for forty years as they stumbled around in the darkness of the desert. They wore their victimization so long it became an identity, so much so that generations later, they even missed God's provision of a promised Messiah.

We're like Israel in a lot of ways, aren't we? We can become consumed with what we need, or want what we don't have, and lose sight of God's constant provisions. So great is His faithfulness to meet our needs that He often meets our needs for years before we recognize the provisions as being from Him. Scripture says that He satisfies our desires with "good" things so that our youth is renewed like the eagle's (Ps. 103:5). Perhaps we need to change our focus. Instead of focusing on the need, let's look with increasing focus on God's provision as He seeks to fill that need His way in order to reparent us into the image of His Son.

The key to this reparenting process is to pay wise attention to those holes or deficits of support in our lives that have been brought about by inadequate parenting and insufficient father support. If, for instance, your father did not provide adequately for your basic physical needs such as shelter, food, clothing, or warmth, it will be important for you to make these needs a central priority in your life. Has God provided or given you the means to meet these needs through a job, money, or source of support? If so, honor those gifts and provisions by using them wisely and then living in an attitude of gratitude that honors your heavenly Father, the provider.

If your father didn't validate your existence or communicate that you were trusted or believed, it will be very important for you to seek out, believe, and receive God's words about you. Some of us stop short in the reparenting process by becoming aware of the need and then looking for the provision in others. We sort of hitchhike, if you will, on God's provision to them. This in turn causes us to become enslaved to others' opinions, approval, and shows of support. We can even end up holding others as emotional hostages in meeting our needs for support, validation, or nurturing. When this happens, we have no chance of complete filling and having our needs met, because we are working off someone else's supply.

Remember, we're all needy in some way, and two people cannot live off the same air supply! How long before someone else's emotional supply runs out with two or more people feeding off it? Then what happens? Right, we look around for someone else. Let's figure it out and go directly to the Source! Only God can sufficiently meet our every need. He is the only one who can fill us up on the inside.

Though He may use other people in the process, these people are only vessels or channels of God's love to us. By making them more, and not recognizing who is the True Provider, we can fall into idolatry, worshiping the created, rather than the Creator.

Let me give you a couple of personal examples of how God has graciously reparented me. I've told you before about my dad's issues with money and how he passed his anxiety concerning financial security on to me. He worked very hard to support my family, but he had a hard time parting with any of his earnings except for food and necessities. As a young child I felt the tension in our home about having enough money to pay the bills. As I said earlier, at the age of 14, I began to work all summer in order to make enough money to buy my own school clothes, just so I could have my own money to control and not have to go through the third degree of having to justify how much money I needed. I still have a hard time asking my husband for money. The words just kind of stick in my throat, but they don't come out. I will even go to great lengths to figure out other ways without having to ask him for money.

It was confusing having money, but not having it, and at times I can still live as if I don't have it. But the Lord has graciously revealed to me that I need to carry cash so that I have a visual reminder that He has provided funds to take care of me. So for several years now, I have carried cash. When I get paid, I go to the bank and exchange the check for cash. This gives me a visual reminder that I'm OK. God has provided. My anxiety goes down, and I actually end up spending less, too!

Also, when I grew up there was no physical affection or "I love you" messages spoken to me at all. Several years ago I took the few childhood photos that depict me being loved by my grandparents and framed them, putting them in prominent places in my house. This way I can look at my inner child all the time and extend love and affection to her.

Now neither of the "reparenting" remedies takes anything away from others in my life. They are simple little things the Holy Spirit has prompted me to do for myself that help support and take care of me. In each of these, God first made provision. He provides my paycheck and He provided the pictures from my childhood. He even gave me the ideas for how I could use them in my life now.

FILLING IN THE HOLES

So how are you doing in identifying those deficit needs in your life? Do your life or your actions reveal you to still be carting around a bulging bag of unmet needs? How does God desire to address those needs? Or is it hard for you to shift these needs to God? After all, we don't actually see Him, so is it reasonable to expect that He will come through for us and meet us at the point of our greatest need? Have you even stopped to ask your heavenly ABBA what His will for you is?

We've all tried the needy route, and we've all tried the over-protected route, and neither of those ways worked, did they? Perhaps God is just what we need. Do you have other people in your life that you depend on to meet your needs more than God? Maybe you look at it in a spiritual way. "God loves me through my wife." OK, I'll buy that to a certain degree. But what happens if your wife has a bad day and she's not very friendly to you, much less loving? Whom do you get frustrated with when your love needs aren't met, your wife or God? Do you say, "God, why don't you love me today?" No, you get angry with your wife. You hold her responsible for loving you and meeting your needs, not God. Yet in reality your wife is a human being, too. She can't possibly meet your needs—she can't even meet her own. She needs a heavenly Father providing for her, too! The point I'm trying to make is first to know who is responsible for your needs: YOU AND GOD. The second point I'm trying to make is the need to balance our dependency on others. Dependency is on a continuum:

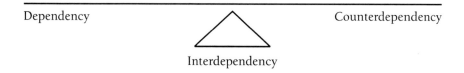

Dependency   Counterdependency

Interdependency

WHERE DO YOU FALL ON THE SEE-SAW OF DEPENDENCY?

Do you hold others hostage to your needs, or do you not need anyone at all? Maybe you can take care of yourself, thank you very much. Or do you allow God to be the source for meeting your needs and recognize His provisions when they come—even when they may not look like a provision. Remember Jesus? He didn't look like Israel expected their Messiah to look, and they missed Him. If your spouse doesn't meet your emotional needs, maybe you've mistaken the provision for the provider! Often, we have to look carefully if we do not want to miss God's gifts to us.

Is there one need on your list that stands out from the rest? Ask God how He wants to fill it. Remember, if we ask for bread, He will not give us a stone. But we do have to be patient and wait for His best.

PEEKING AT THE EFFECTS OF FATHER-WOUNDING ON INTIMATE RELATIONSHIPS

As I've mentioned already, we came into this world dependent on our parents for love and support. When that love and support didn't materialize in the way we needed it, we were left feeling empty and abandoned. As adults, we unconsciously search for someone to fill this empty space in our lives, often believing that our happiness depends solely on being accepted and loved by another person in order to make up our deficit. When we do this, we unconsciously sabotage our best efforts at fostering intimacy with another person. By giving another person responsibility for needs that only we can meet ourselves, we give away personal power and control over our own well-being. We believe we need someone else to complete us. This is a lie that the enemy of our souls wants us to believe.

THE TRUTH, PLEASE

God created us to be complete in Him, lacking nothing except Him. Secular and Christian counselors all agree on one thing—no other human being can make us whole or complete us. Other human beings cannot make up our deficits, and we are not responsible for completing others, either. There is only one: Jesus Christ, who is sufficient to meet all our deepest needs. This is where secular and Christian counselors part company. Our enemy Satan, who is very shrewd and often knows us better than we know ourselves, blends truth and fiction to confuse us. He allows a little truth: others can't meet our needs, and leaves out the truth about the sufficiency of Christ, all the while leading us into temptations that exploit our neediness. That is why many individuals, in unconscious desperation, will settle for temporal substitutes. Settling for a warm body in a relationship seldom works out for our benefit. As long as the fear of abandonment drives us, we are not free to wait on God's best for us.

Though many of us are quite capable of putting on a macho, or self-sustaining veneer, few of us really have it all together. We wear that facade to hide our true fears: that God doesn't have sufficient provision for us, because we are unworthy. In this way, we often take things into our own hands and miss God's best. Remember the case of Abraham? By not waiting for God's perfect promised provision of an heir, he took God's plan into his own hands and created a historical international conflict. That's but one example of the disastrous consequences that we help create for ourselves when we settle for a substitute.

Single individuals often want to marry for the wrong reasons, believing that another can make up for the pain they've suffered and finally complete them. Some even believe that it is the spouse's job to care for the other's unmet needs. After more than twenty-three years of marriage myself, as well as many counseling hours with couples, I can tell you this is a big myth. Believing lies like this is a direct route to holding yourself responsible for responses and needs in others that you have no capacity for fulfilling! I've seen individuals live their lives doing whatever they have to, i.e. having more children than they want, going into debt to keep the other happy, or putting up with abuse or addictive behaviors simply to buy support and commitment. In this way, individuals are often held hostage to meet needs and demands they weren't created to meet. How many divorces take place every day because one or both partners believe the other isn't meeting their needs?

As father-wounded individuals, we have the potential to bring big baggage with us and take hostages wherever we can, and repetitiously repeat empty and aimless patterns that get us nowhere. There is no shortcut to healing. Look at your woundedness. Allow God into those empty and hurting places. Let His words soothe the rawness of your heart. Why stay in the empty preoccupation of our own selves and our own neediness? We don't have to be doomed always to being drawn to those who abandon us like our fathers. The more we allow God to fill those empty spaces with His brand of loving, the more likely we will steer clear of superficial relationships that don't truly meet our needs.

Inadequately fathered men have not learned how to interact with significant women in their lives on an equitable basis. The template for treating women was passed down by the father's example. If dad was distant and emotionally unavailable to his mother, he will treat women in the same way. While he may look like he bonds and relates, it is only a facade to get his own needs met. By example, this is the way his father taught him to relate. Unless a man is willing to learn a more adequate and satisfying bonding process with his heavenly Father first, distancing and hiding will continue to characterize his relationships.

Women with father wounds go through serial relationships like water through a sieve. Deprived themselves of love and attention, they can often shower it on a potential love interest, hoping for a reciprocal effect. She cycles between idealizing the man of her dreams and feeling disappointed and disillusioned that he doesn't love her enough. The ideal man is always just around the corner. These fantasies are born out of a deep-seated wish for a father figure who will finally love and adore her enough. Father-wounded women also have difficulty trusting the love they get when they finally get it. If her worthiness for love was never affirmed by dad, her anxiety and fear that she really isn't lovable at all will fuel clingy, unrealistic demands for love, support, and protection that no mortal man can ever hope to satisfy. Other father-wounded women will run away from very stable, solid men in favor of their familiarity with men who keep them living on the edge like their fathers did.

As you're going to personally experience, father-wound healing can improve us individually as well as in the relationships we value. The more we can acknowledge our spaces of woundedness due to an inadequate connection with dad, the more we are in a position of accepting responsibility for filling those spaces with our own heavenly Father filtered efforts at adequately fathering ourselves. It's a paradox. The more personal responsibility we take in our relationships, the richer our love connections, and the more others will be drawn to us.

TAPPING INTO THE FATHER'S BLESSING

The last area I want to speak to is the Father's blessing in your life. Have you been set free to be an adult? Did your father guide you into that adulthood, or did you just sort of land here without really being equipped for it? Many of us can sense that we're adults on the outside, but we're kids on the inside. Tending to unmet needs by specifically addressing them with God and looking for His provisions will quiet us down and soothe us. Then we have to deal directly with God when we don't like His provision for us, or He's not moving fast enough for us. When you have to face yourself on these issues, you realize who is really in control, and it's not your adult.

We don't demand from God. He doesn't owe us. We owe Him. Let's keep the relationship straight. Yet He still wants to bless us like the Jewish father that He is. He has a legacy that He wants us to take up. Are we willing?

Have you noticed that some people seem to know from the get-go what they want to do in life? However, others of us drift, not really sure whether we're where we're supposed to be or not. It becomes a perpetual search. First, to find something we're good at and like to do, and then to find a place to be able to do it. A good father is an invaluable source in helping his children gain insight into their gifting. He is the coach or the encourager that provides the strong support needed to develop these talents. Unfortunately, many of us have not had the benefit of having had this kind of dad, the kind who invested himself into seeing that we get sufficiently launched in life.

Jeremiah 29:11 says that God has a plan for each of us, a plan for a future and a hope. God has created us with a destiny to accomplish good works for Him, as Ephesians 2:8-9 promises. Due to inadequate fathering, we may have lost our way in finding that destiny, but there is no statute of limitations on God's plan for us. We can still receive the Father's blessing to do what He created us to do. We just need to keep a watchful eye out for insights, talents, and gifts that indicate God's blessing. These can offer us valuable direction. But again, we have to slow down enough to listen.

To tackle this area directly, I'm asking you to quiet yourself before the Lord and ask Him to help you find your direction. Start by focusing on activities you like doing. How do you see God in these activities? Do you see Him using you in this way? Write all this down in a column marked: Activities I Like. Next, has there been any recognition or validation for certain talents or gifts you have? Mark these in a second column entitled: Affirmations. Finally, make a list of your wildest fantasies or daydreams you would like to do, but probably never will. Mark this third list: Dreams. After you've completed these three lists, commit them to God and then let them sit for a month. After a month, review your list and sift it, noting subtle traits, themes, tendencies, or directions that might give you clues about your gifting or your direction. If you need further direction in this area, see the visualization I've included in Appendix C at the back of the book. Remember: "Creativity depends on having the inspiration to do what is already there." Go forth and be inspired!

CHAPTER TEN

Group Study Questions

1. What are the "deficit areas" in your life that need attention? Look over your needs analysis sheet and evaluate whether the way you are meeting your needs now depends on other people in your life or on God.

2. Do you have difficulty receiving help from others? Do you believe you are more prone to dependency or counter-dependency?

3. What are some of the most positive things someone can say to you that feel validating and supportive?

4. Are there needs on your list that God could help you become more responsible for by teaching you how to care for yourself better? If so, in what ways could you take more personal responsibility for these needs?

5. Did you receive your father's blessing to be an adult? How did the blessing or lack of it affect you?

Chapter Ten

Homework Questions

1. In Philippians 4:8-9, Paul writes that we are to focus on that which is true, noble, right, pure, and admirable. If we applied this to facts about ourselves, what facets of your character does the Holy Spirit call you to affirm about yourself. What truths does God want you to know about yourself?

2. What abilities do you have or activities you engage in that affirm God's giftedness in you? Think about those things that you enjoy doing, even if they seem a little crazy to you.

3. What outside recognition or compliments have you received for any of your talents, gifts, or abilities?

4. What are your fantasies and daydreams for yourself, whether they're realistic or not? Maybe you wanted to be a famous ballerina at one time, or a heart surgeon, an evangelist, a skydiver, etc. Write all of your unrealized dreams down, even if they seem outrageous. NAME IT AND CLAIM IT! Remember: Creativity depends on having the inspiration to realize what is already there.

Receiving the Blessing and Mining the Father-lode

Remember the famous Elizabeth Barrett Browning poem, "How do I love thee? Let me count the ways. I love thee to the depth and breadth and height my soul can reach when out of sight..." Have you ever contemplated how much God loves you? Have you ever contemplated how much you love Him? Lovers spend time telling each other how much they love each other. And God spends time telling us how much He loves us. Consider some of His choice phrases to describe His love and regard for us:

> I will rejoice in doing them good and I will assuredly plant them in this land with all my heart and soul.
>
> —Jeremiah 32:41

> You are already clean because of the word I have spoken to you. Remain in me, and I will remain in you. No branch can bear fruit by itself; it must remain in the vine. Neither can you bear fruit unless you remain in me.
>
> —John 15:3-4

> How great is your goodness which you stored up for those who fear you, which you bestow in the sight of men on those who take refuge in you.
>
> —Psalm 31:19

153

Nehemiah said, "Go and enjoy choice food and sweet drinks and send some to those who have nothing prepared. This day is sacred to our Lord. Do not grieve for the joy of the Lord is your strength".

—Nehemiah 8:10

"Am I only a God nearby," declares the Lord, "and not a God far away? Can anyone hide in secret places so that I cannot see him?" declares the Lord.

—Jeremiah. 23:23

Or consider Marie Chapian's personal paraphrase from God to you that incorporates these verses:

To be one with you like this, My child, to hear words of praise from so true a heart, to know these glowing moments when you and I are loving, captivated, engaged in perfect communion—this is the purpose of My Son's death on the cross. He is the link between us; He who opened heaven's walls to let you enter in. Take in My Word: Taste, eat, see and know the heart and mind of God. I am the One who formed you, and breathes breath into your nostrils. I love to accomplish good for you: I give you opportunities like shining halos: take them and be blessed with good. I also give you challenges, unleashed from a sanctuary of bees. Meet them fearlessly because you wear divine protection. I give you the opportunity to know Me and to bless Me, and this is good. Take the opportunity now to bring to Me, like delicacies on a platter, the joy the angels love to see, the joy you were born to know. Come now, let Me hold you near and give you good. Come now beloved, let Me kiss your heart and give you my best.[1]

Now I ask you, couldn't you just bask in that kind of love forever? That's the way our ABBA Father feels toward us. Is that the way we perceive Him loving us? If not, what gets in our way?

Research shows that relationship exists between the way we perceive our parents and the way we perceive God. For example, we know that when we have a marked preference for our opposite-sexed parent, we tend to structure our perception of God to fit this parent. Although these perceptions may fade over time, they rarely disappear altogether.[2] As a result, we can project onto God our deepest needs and He can meet us at our point of need. I would imagine if we took a random survey we could find at least a half dozen or a dozen different stories from all of you that testify to God being the kind of Father who can meet us whatever the need.

The sad thing is that many times we Christians know far more "about" God than we do about experiencing Him as a personal loving Father. Because we can have a tendency to perceive Him through the pigeon hole of our earthly father, we can often "refuse" all that He may have to offer us. C.S. Lewis realized this when he quoted St. Augustine as saying, "God loves where He finds empty hands."[3] A man whose hands are full of parcels or substitutes can't receive what God has to give. He already has his hands full with something else. If we hold onto a misrepresentation of our ABBA Father as depicted by our earthly father, how can God give us His best? Our hands are already full. We can't receive God's loving blessings to us, and we doom ourselves to the bondage of our father-woundedness.

How do we learn to receive? Are you willing to give up the substitutes you've held onto? Can you admit your complete need for His filling? God desires to do this so He can be close with you forever, and so that you would know your inherent worth in Him. Knowing who you are and whose you are can open up whole new vistas in your life to explore without the chains of your father-woundedness sabotaging you at every point. This awareness of your identity frees you from the past to receive grace and forgiveness. Knowing we are accepted unconditionally helps us to turn and give to others in our lives out of the overfill. Isn't it about time that you pulled in for a fill-up?

Now, I have a question for you. Is it possible to practice godly self-love? We hear so much untruth in the world about loving ourselves that sometimes we can end up believing that it is holier and healthier to despise ourself in order to give Christ His due. But how does this negative view of self foster more devotion and love of God if you are so preoccupied with yourself and how sinful you are? That seems to me to be just another form of self-worship of an unhealthy sort.

What does God's Word have to say about us that can give us a view of the Father's perspective? It is very crucial that we have the accurate mind of God about ourselves so that our perspective stays balanced. Here are just a few excerpts from God's Word:

1 Peter 2:9: "But you are a chosen people, a royal priesthood, a holy nation, a people belonging to God, that you may declare the praises of Him who called you out of darkness into His wonderful light." We can say three facts about ourselves in relation to God:

- We are chosen.
- We are a royal priesthood.
- We were created to praise Him and love Him for what He has done for us.

2 Sam. 22:20: "He brought me into a spacious place, He rescued me because He delighted in me." Therefore, I can say:

- God delights in me.
- God rescues me.

Jeremiah 29:11: "For I know the plans I have for you," declares the Lord, "plans to prosper you and not to harm you, plans to give you a hope and a future." Therefore as one of God's children I can say confidently:

- God has plans for me that will give me hope.

Phil. 1:6: "Being confident of this, that He who began a good work in you will carry it on to completion until the day of Christ Jesus." Therefore, I can say:

- I am a person in process.

Romans 8:38-39: "For I am convinced that neither death nor life, neither angels nor demons, neither the present nor the future, nor any powers, neither height nor depth, nor anything else in all creation, can separate us from the love of God that is in Christ Jesus our Lord." Therefore, I can say:

- God is firmly attached to me and will never leave me.

After consideration of all of these Scriptural facts, I think it's safe to say we are loved by a God who has covered all the bases. Indeed, if He loves us this way, then we are lovable and redeemable. Knowing that God extends this love to us like this, I believe our natural childlike response is to drop whatever is in our hands and run to meet Him.

ARE YOU BETTER OFF NOW?

It's important to have an honest appraisal of ourselves by choosing to see ourselves accurately and honoring God's faithfulness to bring us into the freedom He has promised. No, we're not complete quite yet. God is still at work refinishing and honing His creations. But we have to ask ourselves, "Are we better off now than when we were being wounded by our earthly fathers?" Have you overcome your early beginnings with God's help? While there is the need to tend to our sins and scars, there is also the time to enjoy the blessings God has given to us, even in the midst of our painful life experiences, and He has made us complete in Him. Make no mistake. We are not complete because of what we've done, but rather because of what He's done. He's already done the "doing." We are human beings. Therefore we have been blessed to just be.

That's difficult for some of us, me included. It is hard sometimes just to slow down and enjoy the "being." I have a friend I don't see very often anymore. However, when we used to talk more often and I would ask her how she was doing, she would always say, "Blessed. I am so blessed." Back in my "doing" days, I used to hear her say that and think, "Boy, I wish that's all I had to think about." Years later, I realize that's all that's really important, acknowledging the blessings of God and living as a blessed child rather than a forgotten or wounded child.

Can we be content in God's blessing, or does there always seem to be more that is promised or possible just around the corner? The world teaches us to be discontented with who we are and what we have, so they can sell us more things to hold in our hands. If we listen to the world, we will never be enough or have enough. It's called exploitation. The enemy uses the world to exploit us through our discontentment and greed to feel inadequate.

We need to practice affirming our completeness in Christ by challenging ourselves with the realization, "I am enough in Christ. Remaining in Him, I have everything I really need emotionally and physically." It is each of our choice whether we choose to accept the adequacy of God's truth about ourselves. With Christ, we are enough, and everything else that comes our way is just icing on the cake!

MINING THE FATHER-LODE

Have you ever noticed how some of the deepest truths you learn come out of some of the darkest times of your life? Healing your father-wound holds within it many life lessons that you may just now be realizing. In reality, our father-wounds are Father-filtered and bring us a legacy we can use for good in our lives, or for destruction. Strength is often birthed in adversity and challenge. Consider one man's revelation of this truth in his own life.

It's a familiar story in the book of Genesis. Joseph is the favored son of Jacob. So much so that Jacob has a special coat made for him. His brothers become jealous and sell him into Egyptian slavery. You know the story well, I'm sure. Joseph rises to a position of prominence and power in Egypt, for the power of God never leaves him, despite his family's abandonment. When famine comes on Israel, Jacob sends his sons to buy grain in Egypt and they unknowingly come face-to-face with the brother they sacrificed. Joseph readily recognizes them and plays with them for a little while as he gets his emotions under control. Eventually he decides to attempt a reconciliation with them and reveals his identity. Eventually, the family is restored and Jacob dies. Joseph's brothers begin to worry that Joseph may have a change of heart now that their father has died and may want revenge for their former treatment of him. But instead of revenge, Joseph repays their actions out of the overflow of what he has received from God when he says, "Don't be afraid. Am I in the place of God? You intended to harm me. But God intended it for good to accomplish what is now being done, the saving of many lives" (Gen. 45:5).

Joseph had the wisdom to trust God's plans for his life. God used the circumstances of his brothers' sin to save Israel from starvation and to give all of us a picture of wise grace. If you apply Joseph's storyline to your own life, what circumstances from your wounds has God used to direct your life? Perhaps missing out on some part of your father relationship has created a direction for good in the lives of you and others.

In order to ferret out these jewels born in adversity, we need to "mine the father-lode." If we try and reframe our ideas about our past, we may catch a glimpse of the beautiful tapestry God is weaving from the broken parts of our lives. When I use the term the "father-lode," I am referring to the internal strength that has been multiplied within us as we have overcome the deprivation of inadequate fathering. In order to receive the inner strength from this treasure trove we must "mine the father-lode," sifting the jewels or nuggets of value from the dross.

Just like the Japanese create beautiful bonsai creations through the bending and pruning of small trees or plants, the hurt and deprivations of our childhood have yielded special fruit we may yet be unaware of. Jesus assures us of this process in our lives in John 15:1-4 when He promises:

> I am the true vine, and my Father is the gardener. He cuts off every branch in me that bears no fruit, while every branch that does bear fruit he prunes so that it will be even more fruitful. You are already clean because of the word I have spoken to you. Remain in me and I will remain in you. No branch can bear fruit by itself; it must remain in the vine. Neither can you bear fruit unless you remain in me.

Each of us has been shaped by our individual experiences, especially our father-loss experience. Growing up, we may have adopted certain survival-type behaviors to help us get through some tough times. Have those tough times produced any growth in your life to which you can now attest and understand? This is called acquiring the wisdom in the wound.[4] Take a moment and think of as many completions to this statement as you can think of, in order to determine what wisdom in the wound you may have by now.

"Because my dad _____ I _____
_____. I'll share a few of mine to give
you the idea of how the mining process works, in order to find the
wisdom in the wound:

> Because my dad was a workaholic, I have a strong work ethic that
> has led to accomplishments and rewards.

> Because my dad was ashamed of his early beginnings, I moved
> beyond my own.

> Because my dad withheld physical affection and love from me, I
> hug and kiss my children all the time and tell them I love them.

> Because my dad got me the medical treatment I needed as a child,
> I am alive today.

> Because my dad was the only one in his family to graduate from
> high school, I valued and sought after higher education.

Now, it's your turn. List the positive outcomes in your life that
have been born in the pain and adversity of your father-wound.

DEALING WITH THE BY-PRODUCT OF LONELINESS

Some by-products of not having a healthy dad include feelings
of loneliness and abandonment, even emptiness. Very often this
loneliness can seem a trial in and of itself because we are confronted
with our own inadequacies, vulnerabilities, and attachment issues.
We can walk into a crowded room and feel totally alone. At other
times solitude can seem like a menacing presence rather than a
welcome relief.

How do you view solitude? Is it a friend or an enemy? It can be
more than just a trial to get through. Do you use solitude to connect
with your heavenly Father, asking Him to fill you? Have you asked
Him for His thoughts toward you and even written down the impres-
sions you believe He laid on your heart? Can solitude become your
friend, because it signals a time to reconnect your inner spirit with

your Father's? Solitude, though born out of neglect, can be a peaceful friend rather than a dreaded enemy.

Too often, we avoid solitude. We do the "wheelies" of life to avoid dealing with it, filling our lives with too much busyness, responsibilities, and daytimers. We fill up our hands with all sorts of things, such as responsibilities and people. Martha was too distracted by what she had on her hands to seek solitude, but Mary was not. Distractions are everywhere, and they come in every form, such as jobs, computers, children, boyfriends, lovers, money, addictions, or ministry. Anything that is capable of coming between us and spending time with our Father is capable of becoming an idol. Let's empty our hands in order to receive all that God has for us. If you're anything like me, this has to be be a daily choice. I can easily think of a dozen things that have to get done before I can quiet myself before the Lord and allow Him to fill me and touch me. Let's recommit to accepting a Father's unfailing love.

CHAPTER ELEVEN

Group Study Questions

1. Where do you need the Father's blessing in your life?

2. What keeps you from receiving?

3. What "scars" or "bumps" do you carry as a result of your father failing you?

4. Have any of these scars served as unexpected channels to fruitful directions in your life?

5. How has God disciplined or pruned you to grow in His direction, rather than your own?

6. How do you deal with loneliness or disconnectedness?

CHAPTER ELEVEN

Homework Questions

1. Have you received the father's blessing? How has it affected you?

2. Write down three major problem areas in your life or areas of conflict you are now ready to hand over to your heavenly Father. Ask Him to illuminate these areas in different ways so you can see them afresh. Record what He tells you concerning the way out of or through these areas of difficulty in your life. Each day review these problem areas and note any leading from the Holy Spirit as to how you are to respond in these areas of your life for your good. Identify and keep track of blessings He provides along the way.

3. Now examine each of these scars, viewing them from different directions or perspectives. Has God used or worked any of these scars for good in your life? Write as many completions to the following sentence as you can think of:

   Because my dad _____ I _____.

4. If any of these "wisdoms in the wound" have produced blessing in your life, be sure to thank God for His work in your life and His steadfast refusal to abandon you.

The Reconnection Decision

O ver the last few months you have come full circle. Although you may have felt at times as if you were in the desert just like Israel, the time has now come to make some important choices about your relationship with your father. Along the route we have taken together, you have experienced changes that have healed. Some of the changes that reflect God's healing touch on your life have been owning your own woundedness and understanding its long-term behavioral effects. Now you have a more complete perspective of your whole situation. In understanding your anger, you can see both the purpose it serves, as well as the destruction it brings when displaced onto others who aren't responsible for your pain.

You have chosen to forgive your father for some of the past and you have moved from being a hurt child in an adult body to a more healthy, maturing adult in God's kingdom. We have wept together, forgiven together, played together, reflected together, and received the Father's reparenting together in order to reach this day.

You have now come to an important fork in the road of your father-wound healing process. Today is the day you need to make some choices about this relationship that has had an overarching influence on your life. You need to decide what kind of relationship you choose to have with your father from this day forward. Don't worry. It is normal to have some apprehension at this point. Though you do feel stronger on the inside, can you now approach your father as an adult rather than a wounded child? The plan now is to approach your father as adult-to-adult, rather than the wounded child you once were. As a healing adult, you know yourself much better now than when you started this process. The truth is, there really isn't any way that your father can hurt you anymore because you know your vulnerabilities better than he does.

If your dad has already died, he still lives on in your thoughts. As we walk through the options for reconnecting with dads who are still alive, you can also picture yourself making these same choices with your father, even if he is no longer alive. How did you leave your relationship with your dad when he died? How were the two of you getting along and how well did you know each other? These pieces of information will influence the decision you make on this important issue.

Being a reparented adult having a sufficient infilling from your heavenly Father, you can now appreciate all kinds of possible alternatives to reconnect or disconnect with your earthly dad. Though these possibilities may have existed before, it's likely you weren't able to see them as clear, viable options because you were still enslaved to the inner child of your past. No longer are you in bondage to this child's perspective, because you have faced it, accepted it, and allowed your heavenly Father to meet that need within you. That inner child is an integrated part of you now, not the one calling all the power plays behind the scenes. Feeling filled by your ABBA Father and knowing He meets your every need frees you from slavery to one-way relationships. If the truth be known, your heavenly Father has spoiled you for all other relationships, because deeper love and intimacy are possible with Him than with any other relationship you might have.

Having an all-sufficient daddy puts you in the driver's seat about what kind of relationship you will now have with your earthly father. So, what are your choices? The first task we must take up is to determine the right level of contact between you and your earthly father. No longer chained to the past relationship with him, you are free to decide how connected and involved you want to be with him. The options open to you break down like this:

   A. Disconnect from him completely
   B. Accept the relationship the way it is
   C. Build a more genuine friendship with him

Before I develop these three choices in detail for you, I want to sound a cautionary note here. It is not necessary to cultivate a different relationship with your father in order to heal your father wound. The only stipulation is that you accept responsibility for the degree of closeness you choose to have with your dad. This puts your relationship on your terms as an adult, rather than on your father's terms relating to you as his child. Wherever your relationship goes with your dad from this point on, it unfolds as a result of your conscious choice as a an adult, not choices made for you by other well-meaning grown-ups in your past. You now have uncovered all the information you need to make an informed choice about a relationship with your father. Even if your father has already died, I want you to visualize seeing yourself making this grown-up choice about him. It can affect how his memory impacts you. Now, let's turn to the options.

The first option is to disconnect from your dad completely. Many individuals make this choice, because after they look at all the facts and perceptions on both sides, they find their earthly father is not a safe person for them to be around. Consider Josie's story:

Josie had lost her daddy in childhood when her parents divorced and her mother moved her to another state. Several years after Josie had begun receiving counseling as an adult, her father "blew" back into her life. He always seemed to be passing through town with his other family, Josie's stepmother and step-siblings, and he made it a point to contact Josie when they were in town staying at a hotel. He flew her to different locations around the world to be with them on holidays.

Though Josie could be open with her dad about her past, her dad was never able to get beyond a breezy, superficial approach that did not personally disclose himself to her or invite her to be any closer to him. Instead, she got to stand on the sidelines of holiday affairs, watching her father be the center of attention with his other family. These family members often intimately acknowledged that

Josie's dad wasn't able to have deep relationships with them either, but because he liked to be the "big man," gathering all his family members around them—often paying for plane tickets, hotel rooms, and condominiums—they didn't argue.

The last straw for Josie came when her dad wanted her to participate in a "slightly" illegal transaction for his benefit. Josie was horrified and deeply wounded that her father would try to exploit her relationship with him. Since she could never slow him down long enough to talk the situation through to ownership, Josie finally decided to sever contact with her jet-setting dad. She finally saw that she herself was perpetuating her own pain by continuing to respond to her dad's woefully inadequate attempts at relationship. She finally had to accept that despite his displays, Josie really had only a one-way relationship when it came to her dad. He could put on a really good show of connection, but when it really came down to it, Josie was just a human commodity to her father. Trying to relate with her intimacy-avoiding father was like trying to box with someone who wouldn't show up for the match!

Perhaps you live a story like Josie's. No matter how much you try to have a healthy, connected relationship with your dad, it seems you're the only one working. You may have decided after much consideration that your mental, emotional, and/or physical health would be best served in having little to no contact with your father. This can be especially stress reducing if your dad still displays little repentance for past critical/abusive behaviors of you, or still abuses you to this day.

It is not necessary to subject yourself to old abusive and dysfunctional patterns of relating just to stay connected. If you find that trying to communicate with your dad diminishes your dignity and self-worth, choosing to separate can be a healthy decision on your part.

The choice of separation is flexible, permanent, or temporary. You even have the option of taking a "hiatus" from your relationship for six months, a year, etc., to give yourself more time to feel comfortable in using your personal power to have an equitable relationship with him, rather than an unequal relationship that leaves you feeling in the one-down position. I've seen even temporary withdrawal stabilize newfound growth enough to jump-start relationships with fathers later on.

I realize that it takes courage to choose to withdraw from a toxic relationship, especially when you're a Christian. As Christians, we want to obey God's commandment to honor our parents. However, at times we may only be able to practice honoring and respecting them from a distance. To come any closer before we are strong enough to resist their magnetic pull into old dysfunctional patterns of relating can prove to be very dishonoring. By the same token, if you are waiting until you feel "strong and stable" enough to weather the relationships with your father, this may just be an excuse to avoid responsibility of seeing the relationship for what it is.

The second option is to accept the relationship the way it is. Perhaps your father is just not receptive to establishing a closer, warmer relationship, despite your growth and desire to do so. You may need to choose to accept him where he is. If you have genuinely tried to be more open and affectionate with him and he doesn't respond, at least you know you tried your best to move closer to him. Perhaps you will have a relationship with him that doesn't have a great deal of depth. There are some family members I have had to accept by just enjoying a superficial relationship. This may be better than nothing at all in maintaining connections with family members who don't want to move out of their own comfort zones.

By choosing to see what relationship we have in a positive light, instead of comparing the lack of relationship to what other families have, I am freed to move on. They key is in accepting the other person's inability to relate rather than trying to change them.

However, before you choose to accept a relationship "as it is," make sure you aren't choosing this option too easily. Have you honestly tried to disclose yourself to your father? Let me relate a personal story to illustrate what I mean. The first seven years of marriage often hold many trials as two individuals try to forge intimacy by letting each other into their private worlds. I was in the middle of graduate school, married for about seven years, and in the middle of therapy and healing for the emotional baggage I carried from childhood. I remember having this discussion with God about the fact that I didn't believe my husband really knew me, nor did I believe he wanted to know me. As I was lamenting to God about sticking me in yet another one-way relationship, that still small voice spoke to my heart. God asked me, "And whose fault is it that he doesn't really know you?" I was a little taken aback at God's question, because I had been expecting Him to agree with my perspective. But He didn't. In fact, He pursued me further by saying, "Don't you throw away this relationship before you try putting forth the effort to reveal yourself to this man. Don't wait for him to ask you who you are, how you think, what you feel. Tell him! If he rejects you after you've made the effort, then we've got a problem."

At this point now, with more than twenty-nine years of marriage and two children, I am very grateful for God's faithful pursuit and confrontation that day. I could have prematurely given up on a marriage relationship just because I wasn't willing to risk being transparent. But God challenged me to take a risk. It's been one of the best risks I ever took. When I started laying myself out there for my husband to see, I discovered he could handle it, and I believe he enjoyed our differences more than I thought he would.

My point is this: Before you write off a relationship with your dad or anyone else as being too superficial for you, make sure you're not the one running away from going deeper. Even if your dad doesn't like to go much deeper in getting to know you, that doesn't have to stop you from growing. You are not chained to him anymore. Remember, you have a heavenly Father who meets your emotional needs now. How your dad relates to you, good or bad, is about *him*—it's not about you. Just because his inhibitions get the better of him, that doesn't have to bother or offend you, as long as you are letting God help you reparent your needs. If you can allow your dad to be himself, the two of you may be able to take the relationship to a different place.

The last option I want you to consider is the possibility of moving toward a closer connection with your father. Sometimes there are indicators that your dad is ready to move your relationship to a deeper level. Perhaps the man who wasn't able to be a mature father in your childhood may be slightly older and wiser now and can offer you more of his time. Better yet, perhaps as a father or mother to your own children, you have a much better appreciation for the tough job it is to parent and attach to your children effectively. You can now understand with wise grace the difficult stressors your dad faced in fathering you.

This choice to move toward a closer connection must start with you, however. The relationship can only move closer if you're willing to take the first step to being vulnerable, real, and attachable. Be patient with your dad because this change on your part may take him by surprise. Not being as emotionally healed as you, he may be confused by your genuine efforts. However, if you continue to sense an openness on his part to follow you on this new trail of relationship, then help him along by modeling some of the lessons you have learned. While this calls for you to risk being vulnerable and real with him, some dads welcome their adult children's helping them to grow, way into their old age. Take a look at Dennis's story:

Dennis's stepdad was a retired military man. Growing up, heads would roll when Dennis's dad came home at night from the Navy and the home "deck" wasn't spit-shined and swabbed clean. He would start with the oldest, in this case Dennis, and he would go down the line in punishing his "troops" for their irresponsibility. Dennis always got the full force of the beating because he was first. By the time his dad got to the youngest sibling, he was winded and tired, usually barely able to swat the fleeing behind.

As an adult Dennis faced his own inadequacies as a father with honesty and courage. He felt like a child still being responsible for his younger brothers and sisters, without having the big picture. Time spent on his knees before his heavenly Father brought him awareness of his lack of "father training." He was willing to learn a new way of fathering. After watching his own father mellow and shrink with age as he enjoyed his grandchildren, Dennis worked up courage one day to talk with his dad about life as his father's son. To his surprise, Dennis found his dad big enough to admit to a few regrets about his military bearing at home and his lack of tolerance for his own children. His father even cried when he talked about how precious Dennis's children were to him. He said he wished he'd taken the time to enjoy Dennis and his siblings as much as he was enjoying his grandchildren.

Dennis was able to see his dad's heart that day and realized that he could handle one-on-oneness with his dad. That day was a new beginning for Dennis in becoming friends with his dad. He could identify with his dad's fleeting times of tenderness and saw this as being evidence of his father's repentant spirit. Before his dad died, Dennis was able to care for him, and the two of them swapped happy memories. Dennis's dad told him he loved him and that he was proud of the father Dennis had become. Dennis was able to release his father to God, knowing they had reclaimed lost ground in their relationship before he died.

Being healed has its advantages in initiating a closer relationship with your dad. You will have a greater compassion for your father and will be able to meet him half way, inviting him to come into a closer relationship with you. There may be a good chance that he can respond to an invitation that he could not initiate. If there is even a remote chance that the two of you can move closer in these last years, it may be worth a try. Do be aware that the feelings and memories that surface can be strong, so go slowly and savor the moment. After all, you aren't in such a hurry to grow up this time.

The first step to moving toward a closer connection with your father is to initiate the change. This step requires you to accept your father as he is right now, not what you can remold him into. Hopefully, you've released that kind of control by now. This is the person you want to get to know better right now, not a fantasy you want to mold him into for the future.

Initially, you will need to take the first step and change the way you interact with him. All the work you have done to receive God's grace can result in an overfill of grace and compassion to your father. Change the way you talk to him. Attempt to put forth more effort at being warm and making a connection with him, even if it's on a subject he likes. Begin to disclose memories to him, and be sure to tell him thoughts and feelings as he can handle it.

The second step is to establish an equal footing with him. Approach him as another adult in your life, peer to peer. Think about how you would interface with a friend or co-worker on an equal footing, and then act the same way with your father the next time you're with him. Act like an adult peer, and expect him to act like an adult. He may surprise you and rise to the occasion. Rather than asking permission or being in a passive, submissive one-down position, meet him as an equal, expecting him to treat you with the same respect. When it's right, tell him how important it is to you to improve your communication with him. Remember, each of you has his own truth to tell. If you want him to listen to your point of view, then you have to listen to his and try not to correct it. Acknowledge and validate his pain much as you would like him to validate yours.

Finally, there may be an opportunity to talk and clear out the past. At some point in your newfound relationship with your dad, you may wish to tell him about the painful feelings you have had in the past. Be sure to first check out with him whether he is willing to hear these painful feelings and memories. He may not be responsive. Or he may criticize you, deny, or practice selective remembering. Just because he doesn't remember it the same way you do doesn't invalidate what you remember. If he doesn't respond well, thank him for listening and allow him the right to decline this kind of interaction. Remember, he owes you nothing at this point. He is accountable to someone else. Sometimes it is better to capsulize these painful feelings and/or memories into a letter that you do not send, or one that could just be shared with a supportive friend instead.

However, if your dad is willing to listen appropriately, try to stay with the hurt feelings that are under the angry feelings. Staying in your anger will put him on the defensive, and you will end up not sharing the deeper emotions you have. A good formula to use is saying, "When you _____, I felt_____. Keep in mind that the main reason you are sharing these feelings is to put the past behind for both of you so that it doesn't continue to keep a wedge between you. You aren't sharing these thoughts and feelings to gain his acceptance, approval, or validation. You don't need those anymore, because your heavenly Father meets those needs now.

In clearing out the past with your dad, it is important to allow him the freedom to his own perspective. Remember, you can now do this without having to compromise your own. You can use "ands" to connect your perspectives rather than "buts." For instance, "Dad, I'm hearing how frustrated you were in having to be out of a job and responsible for a family, and us kids were feeling hurt because we thought you were angry with us." As much as possible, strive to see things from your dad's perspective.

Find some part of his story you can agree with or validate. This can set the tone for conciliation, rather than further division and detachment. Practice extending the grace that your ABBA Father has extended to you. You have been given so much in His heavenly fathering and adoption, and you can share that with your dad if he meets you halfway. Seeing his perspective is not a transaction or something that requires scorekeeping. It's two sides of the same coin, or two truths. You had the freedom to make your own mistakes, and your dad has the freedom to make his. It takes emotional maturity to let your dad have his own version of reality without your feeling threatened or wanting his approval. Your goal at this point is not to change his mind, but to keep these new communication lines open.

After you have cleaned out as much as you want from the past, it is important to tell your dad what it is you need and want from him now. For some of us, just being able to talk is enough. Others may want on-going family or social involvement. Take the risk to tell your dad that he is special to you and that you enjoy him. Let him know you want him to continue to be in your life. Now that your needs are being met by you and your ABBA, it is very likely that any of your requests of him will come out much less intense and demanding. He may feel more able to meet you on this less intense level.

All the options you have at this point can seem a bit overwhelming. No longer are you in bondage to the child within you that may have wanted to hold onto these wounds. Instead, you are free! You have been freed by an all-sufficient Father who can run circles around any of our earthly dads, even on a bad day!

Part of exercising your choice today involves accepting responsibility for the degree of closeness you choose to have with your dad from here on out. Wherever your relationship goes with your dad from this point on, it unfolds according to your informed choice. For individuals whose fathers have already died, this can affect how his memory continues to impact you.

Part of clearing out the past with your dad is allowing him the freedom to his own perspective. Remember to use the all important "and" to help you keep both perspectives balanced, yours and his. As we learned using the Pillow Exercise earlier, we do not have to invalidate our own perspective to see things from a different perspective. The gain we receive from having both perspectives far outweighs the momentary inconvenience of having to process somebody else's view besides our own.

Accepting responsibility for the closeness you share with your father from this point on requires that you be honest with him about your needs. If he isn't interested, then consider how much of a time investment is healthy for you in this relationship. If your dad is interested in being closer with you, it may require that you make the early attempts to be closer by initiating conversations with him, a hug, looking at old photographs together, or planning a lunch date with him. You make the decisions now, so you make the call!

What If My Dad Has Already Died?

After you've processed all the information regarding the reconnection decision, you may well wonder about its feasibility or application if your father has already died. I was not introduced to father-wound work until my dad had been dead thirteen years. It's a very worthwhile area to explore, so adult sons and daughters can grow up and move on with their lives. All the issues I have covered in the Reconnection Decision are equally applicable here. Though your dad may not be alive, it is necessary for you to mentally picture what choice you would have made concerning reconnecting with him and why you would make that decision. Even now you have a choice about the degree of father awareness you want to have in your life. Here are some suggestions for enhancing your memory of your father:

- Talk to your father internally on a regular basis. Bring problems to him and imagine any advice or direction he might give to you now that he's wiser.
- Write letters to him in a journal such as "Dear Dad: Guess what happened today." If an appropriate time occurs, you may want to give this journal to one of your adult children as a book of wisdom someday.
- Collect physical objects that belonged to your dad or that remind you of him.

- Investigate and search out your father's relatives or his home town, but explore them with his eyes and perspective. What would he see?
- Trace your father's family tree or lineage.
- Visit your father's grave or the place where his ashes were scattered or placed. Mark this in time and place with words of truth and grace about who you've become because of him.
- Design a simple memorial that commemorates your roots as his progeny, such as a box with mementos of him and you, a poem that summarizes your life together or your feelings for him, etc.
- Carry a memento in your wallet or purse that was his so that you touch the physical connection you have with him frequently.

A few summers ago when I visited my mother, she asked me if I would like to have my father's last driver's license. I immediately said yes, and placed it behind my own license in my wallet. Several months later I was teaching another father-wound class and mentioned my mother's recent gift, thinking I would probably come off as too sentimental. I quickly discovered that I wasn't the only one who carried mementos of dad, nor was I the only one with their father's driver's license. I realized that day that not only does carrying that license connect me with my deceased dad, but it connects me with others who are in the healing process.

CHAPTER TWELVE

Group Study Questions

1. What are the changes that have taken place in you in the last three to four months?

2. Share with your small group exactly where you honestly see yourself in reconnecting with your dad. Be ready to own your feelings and thoughts. There is no wrong decision here, unless you're dishonest with yourself.

3. If your dad has already died, how did you leave your relationship with him? How do you feel about reworking your ending with him?

4. If your dad is still alive, do you desire to change anything about the kind of relationship you have with him now? What are those changes?

5. Are there unspoken fears that hinder you from wanting to pursue any change in the relationship? Speak these fears aloud to your small group.

5. What are the pros and cons to changing the level of relationship you have with your dad right now?

CHAPTER TWELVE

Homework Questions

1. If your dad is still alive, how do you feel when you are with him. Do you like yourself when you are with him? Is he a healthy influence in your life?

2. Has your dad made any efforts at repenting from his unhealthy behaviors with you?

3. Have you ever considered taking a vacation or "hiatus" from your dad? Would this help or hurt your relationship with him?

4. Have you ever tried to initiate a change in your relationship with your father? How did he handle your efforts at change?

5. If your father has already died, how would you change the way you left things with him if you could?

6. Create a memorial that commemorates your reconnection decision.

7. Take a look at your notebook from past sessions. What sessions were hardest for you and why? In which sessions did you have the hardest time completing the assigned homework?

8. Which sessions did you work on the hardest? How did these influence your overall healing?

9. Are there individuals in your life who could be healthy father substitutes? If so, who and what contribution do they make to your life?

Healing the Effects of Father-Wounding in Intimate Relationships

If you had to put together a top-ten list of desired qualities in a potential mate, what would it include? When you think of what you would wish for in a life partner, what comes to mind? Take a moment right now and jot down 5 to 10 qualities that would make your all-time top-ten list.

Have you ever wondered why people get married? When I've asked, I get answers like companionship, sharing of lives, creation of a family, or they love each other and want to spend every waking moment together. Oh, if it only stayed that way!

Well, remember God's pronouncement in Gen. 2:18 just before He created Eve. What was it? Right. "It is not good for man to be alone." Attachment is ingrained. God created us with a need to be together.

As I've mentioned before, attachment, according to experts like Drs. Cloud and Townsend, is the foundation of the soul's existence. We've spent many weeks talking about interrupted attachment with our fathers. Part of our healing has been coming to grips with the emptiness our earthly fathers may have passed on to us. You see, a lack of attachment is one of the effects of the sins of the fathers.

Now, I want to give equal time to examining healthy attachment and walk you through what attachment needs to look like if relationships are built to go the distance. Included in your

Stages of Intimacy

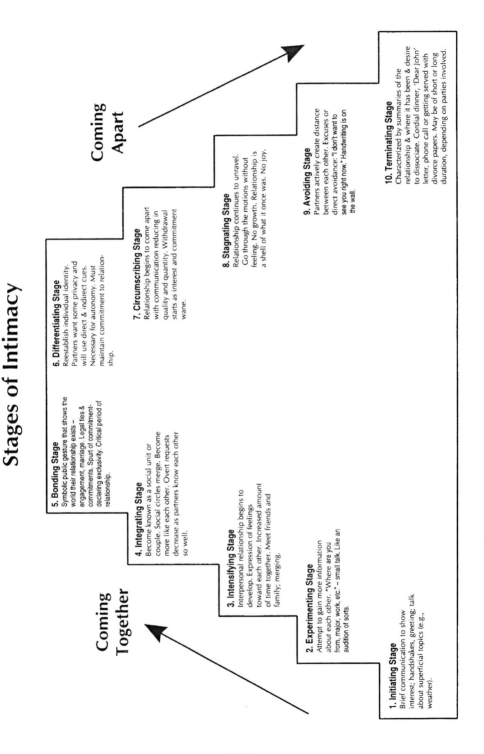

Coming Together

Coming Apart

1. Initiating Stage
Brief communication to show interest; handshakes; greeting; talk about superficial topics (e.g., weather).

2. Experimenting Stage
Attempt to gain more information about each other. "Where are you from, major, work, etc." – small talk. Like an audition of sorts.

3. Intensifying Stage
Interpersonal relationship begins to develop. Expression of feelings toward each other. Increased amount of time together. Meet friends and family; merging.

4. Integrating Stage
Become known as a social unit or couple. Social circles merge. Become more like each other. Overt requests decrease as partners know each other so well.

5. Bonding Stage
Symbolic public gesture that shows the world their relationship exists – engagement; marriage. Legal ties & commitments. Spurt of commitment-declaring exclusivity. Critical period of relationship.

6. Differentiating Stage
Reestablish individual identity. Partners want some privacy and will use direct & indirect cues. Necessary for autonomy. Must maintain commitment to relationship.

7. Circumscribing Stage
Relationship begins to come apart with communication reducing in quality and quantity. Withdrawal starts as interest and commitment wane.

8. Stagnating Stage
Relationship continues to unravel. Go through the motions without feeling. No growth. Relationship is a shell of what it once was. No joy.

9. Avoiding Stage
Partners actively create distance between each other. Excuses or direct avoidance: "I don't want to see you right now." Handwriting is on the wall.

10. Terminating Stage
Characterized by summaries of the relationship & where it has been & desire to dissociate. Cordial dinner, 'Dear John' letter, phone call or getting served with divorce papers. May be of short or long duration, depending on parties involved.

workbook is a stair-step diagram that depicts the Stages of Intimacy in relationships.[1]

I will summarize them here as you look at the diagram. The left side of the diagram depicts the stages of relationships coming together. I jokingly refer to this side as the Stairway to Heaven. The right side of the diagram depicts the stages where relationships unravel or come apart, and the sober reality is that this side represents the Stairway to Hell. Interestingly enough, I have watched these stages operate in all kinds of relationships, including family, roommates, and same-sex friendships. Relationships don't have to have a romantic or sexual element in them to develop intimacy. As intimacy develops in any relationship, there are characteristic stages the relationship will move through. Let's walk through these stages together:

INITIATING: The initiating stage is where two people meet. They exchange small talk about topics that are external to them in which they have no personal investment, i.e. the weather, the price of peas, etc. This stage can last five minutes or longer depending on the circumstances. Once the conversation turns to exchanging more personalized information, the relationship moves to the next stage.

EXPERIMENTING: This stage can take more time than Initiating. I like to compare it to my personal hobby of fishing. The parties involved are actively throwing out their lines to see if they get a bite and some common interest is established. Now, this stage is still fairly superficial because as people try out for the part of being a friend, they usually will try to put their best foot forward, and some will even be dishonest in doing so. It's important to be aware that you will only see what that other person wants you to see and vice versa.

INTENSIFYING: Once a friendship where two people are participating and investing themselves in connecting with each other on an increased frequency begins to develop, the relationship should slowly intensify. As increased amounts of time are spent together, emotional and physical intimacy can develop. It's important to note that especially in romantic male-female relationships, intimacy develops differently. Females desire emotional intimacy before physical intimacy. When women feel emotionally secure and safe, they will naturally move to more deepened expressions of physical intimacy. However, men are different. They see physical intimacy as a direct route to building emotional safety and security in a relationship. It seems very natural to a man that to build intimacy and closeness, he must be physically close.[2] This difference between genders has been the source of many misunderstandings and premature sexuality in relationships. When relationships rely on physical closeness outside the bounds of marriages as the main expression of their intimacy, emotional security and safety within the relationship is sabotaged.

It is especially important for father-wounded individuals to recognize the reality of intimacy differences. Because of the deficit of a father's emotional connection and love, we are often vulnerable to sex-for-love transactions. The stage of intensifying needs to be expanded to run its full course, so families and friends have the time to merge and get to know each other. Individuals need to see each other's reactions in a variety of settings over time to get an accurate picture of the total person. With the divorce rate at an all-time high in the nation, and even slightly higher among Christian couples, taking the time to allow God to build intellectual, emotional, and physical intimacy on His timetable is an absolutely essential ingredient for relationships that go the distance.

INTEGRATING: Once a friendship or romantic relationship has declared a commitment of exclusivity, i.e. best friends or not dating other people, etc., the relationship begins to integrate. The relationship begins to be known as a unit, as you don't see one of the parties without the other. Friends and family become well acquainted and may even form friendships amongst themselves. One word of caution here is that direct verbal communication can actually diminish as two individuals get to know each other so well they can finish each other's sentences. Too much of this kind of similarity can fuel the myth of mindreading that can often sabotage newly married couples. Though partners often enjoy anticipating each other's needs during courtship, it's an unsustainable practice for the duration of a relationship. Sooner or later, individuals must start stating their needs and wants aloud again if the relationship is to genuinely mature with two healthy individuals within it taking responsibility for themselves.

BONDING: This stage in intimacy development is characterized by some sort of public gesture or legal contract that tells the world they are a unit, such as engagement, marriage, two roommates signing a lease together, etc.

Many relationships race through these first five stages of intimacy. Generally speaking, true intimacy isn't something that can be rushed. Relationships that spend at least two years from Initiation through Bonding set the best foundation for stability. The next stage of differentiation will test that stability, and if the relationship has not established enough depth over time, the relationship can begin to slide down the slippery slope to termination.

DIFFERENTIATING: Sooner or later one or both individuals in any relationship will feel the need to stretch and grow, looking outside the relationship in order to meet human needs for intellectual and emotional stimulation. No relationship can ever meet all of a person's needs, because none of us is capable of taking care of anyone else besides ourself.

This differentiation is actually a very healthy stage in the relationship, although initially it can be perceived as threatening. Differentiation will bring new life and fresh perspective back to the relationship, causing it to grow in breadth and depth. However, if either of the parties is threatened by this differentiation, the relationship may stay stifled or stunted for a while until emotional maturity grows.

Practically speaking, differentiation begins to take place when one partner looks to changing their lifestyle, such as going back to school, work, changing jobs, etc., almost anything that brings the influence of the world outside the relationship into the relationship. The key to a healthy balanced relationship is to keep the dynamic tension maintained between Bonding and Differentiation.

CIRCUMSCRIBING: This stage begins when differentiation is allowed to go unchecked and the parties in a relationship start losing touch with each other. The key to recognizing this stage is a change in the frequency and quality of communication. Distraction and withdrawal away from the relationship are common. Wise relationships recognize this red flag and choose to revert back to behaviors that were more common to the Intensifying through Bonding stages. This choice helps the relationship recapture former levels of intimacy, i.e. having a weekly or bi-weekly date night, or having a daily quiet time together just to stay caught up and attuned to each other. Relationships that ignore this time of alert will slip further down the slope to the status quo of stagnating.

STAGNATING: This phase is characterized by a feeling of numbness and automatic behaviors. The relationship looks the same on the outside, but inside there's emptiness, and individuals exist in quiet despair as they go through the motions of maintaining a good front. Much like a stagnant pond with no fresh water source begins to stink and dry off for lack of reinvigoration, the stagnant relationship is a shell of what once was.

AVOIDING: Partners in this phase make conscious choices to avoid the other. In a friendship, longer and longer periods go by without contact. Roommates make choices to come home only when they know the other person is not around. Spouses spend many nights away from home, or come home just to sleep at night. Relationships often exist in this stage for years, because neither party is willing to step up to the plate and call it what it is for fear of being the bad guy. Consequently, the relationship stays stuck until the pain of staying in the relationship outweighs the fear of leaving it. The avoiding phase in a relationship tends to narrow the options as partners increasingly see only one way out, and that is termination. By this time, most partners are too empty to want to go back to any earlier stage in the bonding process.

TERMINATING: This stage is characterized by a departure or final formal dissolution of the relationship. It may be a Dear John or Dear Jane letter, getting served with divorce papers, or coming home to an empty apartment. Either way, there is usually some act that signals a closed chapter to this relationship.

THE ORIGINS OF DEFENSIVENESS

Father-wounding can sabotage our ability to have what we want the most, to love fully and unconditionally and to receive full and unconditional love. Over the years it's quite likely that we've developed certain protective strategies that, while they may keep us from getting hurt, may also keep others from getting as close to us as we would like. It's a relational paradox. The very things we need the most, such as love and acceptance, we can actually repel with behaviors that are intended only to protect us. What am I talking about? I'm talking about defensiveness. Defensive strategies are aimed at keeping out the bad while letting in the good. The only problem is, in our abundant desire to protect ourselves at all costs, we can end up doing just the opposite: keeping out the good while letting in the bad. To understand how this confusion takes place, let's look at the problem from the beginning.

As children, defenseless and uninformed about the world, it was very natural for us to turn to our "daddies" for nurturing and protection. God made us that way. Unfortunately, sin, with its mark upon the world, hampered many fathers from giving proper support, acceptance, and approval. The result is that we feel an emptiness where a resource of inner, personal support should be. As adults, we often search consciously or unconsciously for someone external to fill this empty space. When we find this someone, we believe we will finally feel happy.

Now, for those of you who are married or who have been married before, or perhaps have been in a close, intimate relationship for a long period of time, I have a question: Did having that person in your life live up to your expectations for true happiness? If you're like most of the audiences I've surveyed, the answer is an unqualified "No."

You see, while God has created us with the innate need to attach together, it is not because we are incomplete. We are God's crowning achievement in creation. We are created in His image, lacking nothing except to need Him. The mark of sin has marred this sense of completeness, so that we often become confused about feeling complete.

While we yearn and groan for unconditional acceptance by those around us, deep down inside we question whether we are truly worthy of the approval and acceptance we seek. In our desperation, emotional pain, and confusion about our needs, we can often settle for "temporal substitutes." Something we can stick in the emptiness for a little while, at least, to relieve our confusion and desperation. If we can "believe" even for a little while, that our emptiness is filled, we can survive.

The more we despair, the less selective we can become about our choices to fill this emptiness. This leads us to becoming entangled with people or friends who are not right for us, because inside we despair of ever finding someone to complete us. There's a seed of truth in this despair. There is no one this side of heaven who has the capacity to fill us and completely make up for our unmet needs. I see many people who get married believing the lie that finally, this person will make them happy. Too often, within a few years they begin to discover the sad but true reality that happiness, contentment, and fulfillment of unmet needs does not come in the form of another human being. Often though, this truth is ignored as the search begins anew for a new person to put in the empty hole. And so the pattern repeats itself.

TRUTH VS. LIE

The lie that is perpetuated is this: Completed happiness lies out there somewhere in someone or something.

The truth is: We are complete in Christ—lacking nothing, except what He provides.

Now, perhaps you're sitting there thinking, "I know that. Tell me something I don't know." And my question to you is, "Do you really?" Has the truth descended the 18 or so inches from your head to your heart? Do you live it and walk it out every day? I don't know about you, but I see a lot of despair and loneliness in people, single and married. I believe it's a part of the human condition—not necessarily the direct result of having the right person in your life. Experiencing this despair can lead people to "settling" for second best. We put up with chaos in relationships, crazymaking behaviors, infidelity, addictions, etc., you name it, just to make sure we're not alone. Do you think this is what God meant when He said, "It is not good for man to be alone?" I must confess to you that I have my doubts. Somehow we've gotten off the mark. We've confused our unmet needs with God's plan for lifetime companionship.

As followers of the Good Shepherd, we are challenged from time to time about the dumbness of sheep. Many times we follow our old patterns because we don't know anything else. What about getting rid of the "lie" once and for all. Instead of seeking for someone to make you happy, which we now know is impossible—why not wait for God's best?

While you're waiting for God's best, you need something to do. Take a look at your top-ten list of potential qualities. Interestingly enough, these qualities can act as a mirror, because they are precisely the same qualities you need to foster in yourself to feel complete.[3] Think about it for a moment before you throw what I just said out the window. Try turning one of these qualities around. Say you wrote down "integrity" as a quality you desire in a potential mate. How are you doing in this area of your life? Do you need more integrity in your life? How can you get that? What about companionship—someone to share your life with. How are you doing in that area? Are you truly sharing yourself with others, as you walk through life—or are you holding back, fearing rejection? Are you spending enough time alone, getting to know and accept yourself as God sees you? Or do you run from that alone time and fill it up with work or friends or other habits?

BUILD A NEW HABIT

Practice using the phrase: "If I had more _____ myself, then I would no longer need to _____," for each of the qualities you wrote down.[4]

Father-wounded individuals often do not have sound role models to pattern after in relationships. Many times we have to feel our way along in growing closer to people, simply because we don't know what real closeness feels like. Once the excitement, fantasy, and wonder have worn off of a new relationship, we don't know what to do next. The more we can acknowledge the "spaces" of woundedness in our lives, the more we open ourselves up to accepting personal responsibility for filling up those spaces with our own God-breathed brand of fathering and setting the stage for richer love connections in the future.

Turning now to a different piece of our father-wound legacy, have you ever wondered about the difference in investment people put in when they are looking to get married? Sometimes our wagon gets hitched to the goal alone, without taking the time to weigh what it will exact from us once we have it.

Recently while driving together, my husband and I mused out loud whether people nowadays work as hard to stay married as they do to get married in the first place. For myself, I remember I didn't have a clue at the time. Getting married was the goal. How I've managed to stay that way for almost thirty years is a miracle, considering how totally unprepared I was. The most I can say is that God used what little we brought to the table and over the years has equipped us with the tools, and integrity to use those tools, and has kept us working at it. The power behind those resources rests totally with God. If I had it to do over, I think I could've prepared better for this lifetime journey. I could have equipped myself with more awareness and resources. But I stand in awe of the faithfulness of my heavenly Father in meeting my needs with perfect provisions to build a healthy relationship.

Can I issue a challenge to you? At this point you are in the position to either right the love relationship you are in or to prepare yourself to recognize the right relationship when it comes your way. Singles can often feel anxious between relationships. It is normal to feel good in the early stages of a relationship when we see the other person's interest in us growing. But actually, high-quality love demands just the opposite. If we can receive God's love for us as we are, we can create a new standard of love relationship for ourselves. Loving by this standard accepts no substitutes. Loving and appreciating God's work in us demands high-quality love in return. Respecting a person, whether it be their personhood, their achievements, their character qualities, etc., is the precursor for high-quality love. You cannot truly love a person you do not respect. If you respect yourself, you will attract others who respect you.

Along with the legacy of lacking attachment capabilities, father-wounded individuals also have difficulties communicating. Developing transparency in communication is a worthy quality to grow in relationships that are thriving and growing. However, being transparent requires courage and openness. In Matthew 7:3-5, Jesus spoke of the obstacle that thwarts transparency:

Healing the Effects of Father-Wounding in Intimate Relationships

> And why do you look at the speck that is in your brother's eye, but do not notice the log that is in your own eye? Or how can you say to your brother, 'Let me take the speck out of your eye,' and behold, the log is in your own eye? You hypocrite, first take the log out of your own eye, and then you will see clearly to take the speck out of your brother's eye.

Transparency requires us to take the log out of our own eye before we try to remove the speck in someone else's. Too often, transparency is cast aside for the safer quality of defensiveness. To be defensive means to cover up—to thwart an offensive move. Don't you just love it when people tell you, "Now don't get defensive...." Have you ever wondered how they know you're going to get defensive? Most likely because they feel defensive in the first place, and they assume you will too.

Defensiveness started in the Garden of Eden with the first alibi. Remember, God asked Adam why he ate the fruit from the forbidden tree. He didn't ask Eve. Don't think for a moment God didn't already know who ate it first. Yet what does Adam do? He says, "Yes, but it was the woman you gave me who brought it to me and I ate it" (Gen. 3:12), implying that it was ultimately God's fault for giving him the woman who gave him the fruit. Here is where "defensiveness" entered the human race. As long as sin is on the earth, we will have a choice to be defensive and try to cover up our spaces and shortcomings, or be transparent and tell the truth.

The following table lists some of the protective maneuvers many of us go through to avoid being open and transparent about what we really think and feel:[5]

As you can see, when our loved ones hold those reflective mirrors up, our first level of response is either to attack or blame the other person, distort the information they give us, or avoid why they say it all together. None of these responses is healthy, but they all are normal in that all human beings practice them in order to cope and protect themselves. However, if we are submitted to the Holy Spirit's work in our lives, we can have the safety net of working outside our comfort zone, occasionally entertaining input from others that we do not relish hearing. God often speaks to us through others to get our

Getting Defensive!

Defensive Communication Styles:

Attack The Critic:
  Verbal aggression
  Sarcasm

Distort Critical Information:
  Rationalization
  Compensation
  Regression

Avoid Dissonant Information:
  Physical avoidance
  Repression
  Suppression
  Apathy
  Displacement

Non-defensive Strategy:

1. Seek more information, i.e. description or examples of offensive behavior, consequences for them, what they want, anything else wrong.
2. Find something they've said that you can agree with like a behavioral fact or a perception.
   Agree with this—validate their concern before explaining your own.

attention, helping us see the prism of our own lives so we can hold onto that which is good and modify that which needs repair.

Faithful are the wounds of a friend.

—Prov. 27:6

Iron sharpens iron, so one man sharpens another.

—Prov. 27: 17

Adopting the two-step approach of seeking more information and agreeing with our critic in handling defense-provoking situations will allow others to be in relationship with us with less fear, while still serving to defend us from unjust or unnecessary attacks.

I find that most individuals just want their point of view heard by another person when they communicate, rather than seeking complete agreement. Practicing a non-defensive style of communication creates emotional safety between two people who desire deeper intimacy. This may be frightening at first for a father-wounded individual who has had no real-life example. A good father, like your ABBA, provides not just a tool, but abundant training time in learning to use the tool. Ever-deepening relationships provide us with continued opportunities to take God up on His father-faithfulness.

LEARNING TO USE THE LANGUAGE OF RESPONSIBILITY

In coming to a place of taking more responsibility to communicate effectively in order to foster healthy connections, I have found that learning to use the all important word "I" to start sentences is absolutely necessary. In fact, it's the only time we can talk about ourselves with others and not run the risk of being self-centered! Learning to use "I" language helps define us to others. Learning to use I think, I feel, I believe, I wish, I want, rather than "You" language or even "It" language builds emotional safety into relationships, because we know where the other person stands. We know what their boundaries are because we stumble over them in ignorance. Using the tool of "I" language is a proactive step in building healthy communication. I've included a table to help you grasp the basics of this kind of communication so you can start building richer connections with those you love and stem the tide of father-wounding to the next generation.

THE LANGUAGE OF RESPONSIBILITY

"I" Statements

"I" statements take ownership for what you are saying. Use I think, I feel, I believe, I like, I want, etc. Using the all important "I" defines who you are and where you stand. Using "I" language usually results in your message being heard better and longer. In addition, remember that feelings are one word, i.e., I feel happy, I feel confused, I feel frustrated.

Using the phrases "I feel that you..." or "I feel like it should..." are inaccurate and counterfeit feeling statements because they are really thoughts being disguised in feeling language. These counterfeit feeling statements confuse listeners about where you stand and what you really feel.

"It" Statements

"It" statements allow you to avoid taking responsibility for what you think, feel, believe, want, etc. "It" attributes responsibility to some unidentified, vague source.

Examples: "It seems to me..." "It would be best..." "It's a lot harder to..."

"You" Statements

"You" statements express a judgment on the other person, even if it is only implied, i.e., "That was a stupid thing to say... or "Don't be so critical..."

"You" statements provoke the most defensiveness in others. As people become defensive and protective of themselves, they listen less to what is actually said.

"We" Statements

"We" statements allow you to share ownership whether the other person wants to or not. "We" statements can be used as a transition point in moving from "it" and "you" statements to "I" statements.

There are three parts to a complete "I" statement:

a. describe the behavior of the other person

b. tell them your feelings (remember feelings are usually one word)

c. the consequence their behavior has for you

194

Healing the Effects of Father-Wounding in Intimate Relationships

Precise Language

High-abstract language is vague, unclear, and equivocating. The listener will not be clear on your meaning.

Examples: "Thanks for cleaning up." "Give me a haircut." "Please service my car." "Can you keep my child?"

Low-abstract language gives much more detail and spells out your desires, wishes, and expectations much better.

"Thanks for washing the dishes, vacuuming, dusting, and doing the laundry."

"Please take an inch off the ends."

"The brake pads on my car need servicing. Call me if you find something else."

"Can you come over to my house and watch my two-year-old on Friday night from 8 P.M. to midnight, feeding him dinner and making sure he is in bed by 9:30 P.M.?"

"But" Sandwiches

"*X* but *Y*" makes for confusing statements. "But" tends to cancel out the thought that precedes it. A speaker tries to hide the negative thought between more positive thoughts.

Example: "This story is good, but it could use more creativity."

Instead: "Your storyline is a good one. Is there any way you could develop the main character's personality some more?"

Make each statement short and make it stand on its own. Try using "and" to connect your thoughts rather than "but."

Counterfeit Questions

Counterfeit questions ask a question that is really a statement or that hides your real agenda.

"What's for dinner...what are you doing tonight...can you do me a favor...have you finally finished the dishes...are you going to give him what he deserves this time?"

These are really statements of what you think or want, rather than sincere questions. Using these kinds of statements helps the speaker avoid taking responsibility for self-thoughts and expectations.

Powerless Language

Hedges: "I'm kind of disappointed.

Hesitations: "Well, we could try that..." "I wish you would try to be on time."

Tag questions: "It's about time to get started isn't it?" "You left him, isn't that right?" "You were angry, right?

Disclaimers: "I probably shouldn't say this, but..

SAY WHAT YOU MEAN AND MEAN WHAT YOU SAY. IT'S NO FUN TO TRY AND CONNECT THE DOTS IN COMMUNICATION.

CHAPTER THIRTEEN

Group Study Questions

1. What personal needs do I transfer into intimate relationships? Are any of these needs my personal responsibility to address?

2. What are some of the myths or lies that I have bought into concerning intimate or romantic relationships? Have I paid the cost yet for believing these lies?

3. How's my attachment capability?

4. What's my defensive style of relating to others when they try to tell me information I don't want to hear about myself?

5. Which style of communication am I better at: "I" language, "You" language, or "It" language?

CHAPTER THIRTEEN

Homework Questions

1. In what ways have I either actively or passively expected others to meet my personal needs for love, security, or support?

2. Are there any of these personal needs that I'm willing to accept responsibility for now?

3. If you haven't already, please list ten potential qualities you would like to have in a mate. Maybe some of them are present in the mate you have now, if you're married. Some of these qualities may also be ones that are not present in your significant other.

4. If you used these ten qualities you just listed as a mirror of yourself, what areas need to be encouraged and fostered in your own life? Example: If I list *honesty* as a desired quality in a mate, is it possible that I need to be more honest with others about what I really think, feel, or do? The ten qualities we most desire in others usually are a reflection of areas of need within ourselves that we are looking for others to complete.

5. What new behaviors will I practice in my present or future intimate relationships that address these needs? (Be sure and make it an observable behavior, so you will know that you are indeed making the change.)

6. How will I pace my relationships now that I know what needs to be happening at each stage of intimacy?

7. Practice turning this phrase around: If I had more_____ _____ myself, then I would no longer need to _____.

Trigger Is Not a Horse

This week I want to continue with the idea that partners and even potential partners can be a reflection of ourselves. The significant people we choose to love and live with often bring out our true talents and gifting and can encourage us to reach our true potential. However, it is often true that those things we dislike about our mates can show us aspects about ourselves that we often ignore or deny. The traits in others that bug us the most can call our attention to the very areas within ourselves that are unresolved, fearful, and/or still hurting. This is very likely a description of the human predicament Jesus talked about in Matthew 7:3-5, which we also looked at in chapter 13:

> And why do you look at the speck that is in your brother's eye, but do not notice the log that is in your own eye? Or how can you say to your brother, 'Let me take the speck out of your eye,' and behold, the log is in your own eye? You hypocrite, first take the log out of your own eye, and then you will see clearly to take the speck out of your brother's eye.
>
> —NASB

When we hotly point our finger in condemnation at another for what they are doing, we often reveal the unspoken truth about ourselves. Over-reactions to others' behaviors can very often expose our own unfinished business with our past or with ourselves.

As Jesus pointed out, it is our tendency to always assume the cause of trouble is "over there." "It's your problem, not mine." However, trying to separate ourselves from our "chosen" (by us) life partner can be as fruitless as trying to cut off noses we don't like. In marriage and significant relationships, our intimates hold up mirrors that reveal our unacknowledged dark sides.[1] Oftentimes, what we hide from ourselves, the people closest to us will display. What we suppress, they will express. If our mate has a temper tantrum, then some part of us carries pent-up anger or rage, despite seeming composure. Those closest to us can lay bare our open wounds to others by their behavior, just as we can lay open theirs.

Separation and divorce do not rid us of these reflections, because we will only find other mirrors. What we disapprove of in our mates can clarify what we have to accept or modify within ourselves. In other words, through their reflection, they can disclose us to ourselves. What we cannot or refuse to see within ourselves, they unconsciously put right in front of our faces.

To help prepare us for these inevitable revelations, it is important to understand the nature of conflict better. Conflict is a natural part of life, especially with those we love. A wise man I know puts it this way: "We are always in one of three places at a given time. We are either leaving a problem, in the midst of dealing with a problem, or coming up on a problem!"[2]

Conflict is as natural as breathing. However, it scares most of us to death! When we encounter conflict in an intimate relationship, the automatic tendency is to think, "This shouldn't be happening. If we really were right for each other, we wouldn't disagree." If it's true that partners will never disagree in a healthy relationship, then let me suggest to you that one of you is unnecessary in the relationship.

You see, conflict is beneficial and one of the greatest tools God uses to refine our character and maturity. What is it that James says? "Consider it all joy, my brethren, when you encounter various trials, knowing that the testing of your faith produces endurance" (Jas. 1:2-3).

Perseverance through storms in relationships can reveal new insights, new boundaries, and hidden gifts. Knowing you can work through and survive conflicts in relationships extends the roots of that relationship even deeper, ensuring greater stability. Being able to work through conflicts successfully, however, depends on the participants' willingness to tell each other the truth. Quarrels are seldom altogether about the supposed objection at hand. Rather, they are more about the unmet needs or the underlying fault lines that lie within our individuality that we strive to conceal.

All of us have a specific conflict style that we use to navigate the waters of life's inevitable conflicts. Some of us have styles that are more effective and functional than others. First, let's consider the non-assertive style:

NON-ASSERTIVE: These individuals are unwilling or unable to express their needs, thoughts, and feelings directly. Instead, they deal with the inevitable conflicts that arise in relationships in one of two ways: avoidance or accommodation.

DIRECT AGGRESSION: With direct aggression, the individual makes demands or tries to control the other's movements in ways that threaten the other person's presenting self.

PASSIVE-AGGRESSION: A very common, but deadly, way to deal with conflict by dealing with conflict in an obscure or underhanded way.

CRAZYMAKING: Crazymaking behavior is actually a subset of passive-aggressive behaviors, which allow one individual to express feelings of hostility or rage in indirect ways, while maintaining a facade of kindness and blamelessness. (See Table for specific Crazymakers.)

INDIRECT COMMUNICATION: Indirect communicators do not feel comfortable bringing a subject up directly. Instead they talk about it in a vague, indirect fashion causing you to have to "connect the dots" if you want to get the picture.

ASSERTION: Assertive individuals are able to express their needs, thoughts, feelings, and opinions without judging or dictating to others.

Next time you find yourself upset or your insecurities are triggered by a loved one, try to understand what God may be showing you about areas He still wants to touch. Instead of allowing the other person to push your panic button, use your rising indignation as an opportunity to observe and work through deeper levels of your father-loss. Many times when we are honest with ourselves, we find that the intensity of the response we feel does not match the present provocation.

Father-wounded people tend to overreact to current pain and stimulation because it reactivates unmended emotional injuries. Maybe your partner is triggering your sense of childhood neglect, or a supposed flaw you were criticized for as a child. You can feel trapped, abandoned, and exposed in a split second. It has been speculated that triggers that disturb us tremendously are about 58% due to traumas before the age of six and 40% due to later events that replicate these original painful situations.[3] Triggers help to identify the tip of our icebergs when present day circumstances connect to submerged anger and pain of the past.

When you are able to see that triggering incidents give you a clear picture of your past, you can use the direct access their revelations afford to mine the wisdom in the wound. The key to remember is this: Your partner's characteristics are just the spark, not the source of your pain. When you are in the midst of an argument, try to make the connection to what earlier pain is being triggered. In this way, your overreactions can speed your growth rather than hinder it. Using these triggers can give you the opportunity to challenge and release outdated attitudes and beliefs that you are holding onto that no longer work well for you. In this way, you can construct a more stable emotional foundation for yourself than your earthly father gave you. Try this clarification dialog the next time you find yourself overreacting with a significant person in your life:

> "Can I share with you why I got so upset yesterday when we talked. It really has very little to do with you. It has more to do with me and my issues. I want you to know this about me so that you can feel safe with me. When you (behavioral statement), I thought (possible interpretation). I felt _____." Then tell them how similar situations in the past have helped to create these interpretations and feelings, making sure that you take responsibility for holding on to them and keeping yourself in bondage unknowingly.

DANCING THE SAME OLD WAY

As we've seen, growing up father-wounded can direct our lives in very familiar paths, if not always satisfying ones. Growing up wounded causes us to adapt survival skills that may have served to fill empty areas and protect us from getting re-wounded the same old way. However, when those survival skills become so pronounced that they are our primary modus operandi, we run the risk of attracting individuals who are just like the fathers and offenders we're running from. One of the most common paradigms to watch in relationships is the Overfunctioning-Underfunctioning Dance. If you've experienced this dance first-hand or seen it exhibited in others, you know the ingenious and seemingly magnetic attraction these two people have for each other. I've listed below the dance steps for each:

Overfunctioner's Steps	*Underfunctioner's Steps*
1. Controlling: Knows what's best for everyone.	1. Doesn't take responsibility for self or anyone else.
2. Quick to advise, fix, rescue or take over.	2. Reluctant and indecisive.
3. Can't handle seeing others struggle, materializes: Unconsciously robs others of their right to grow.	3. Helpless: Afraid of making a mistake. Would rather others take the risk of being responsible.
4. Focuses on others' problems as a way of avoiding personal needs.	4. Seen by others as helpless, needy, dependent, and draining.
5. Hides vulnerabilities under façade of strength and "togetherness."	5. Sees self as a disappointment.
6. Vulnerable to misuse because they're viewed as "always reliable."	6. Uses vulnerabilities to draw others to take responsibility for them.
7. Togetherness attracts and encourages underfunctioning behavior in others.	7. A. Others distance themselves or enable. B. Neediness attracts overfunctioners.
8. Has difficulty "receiving."	8. Has difficulty "giving."
9. Struggles with anger/resentment/depression.	9. Struggles with bitterness/inadequacy/failure/burnout/depression.
10. Hides vulnerabilities out of fear of abandonment.	10. Hides competencies for fear of abandonment.
	11. Undefined, allows others to steal their voice, will, dreams

RESISTING CHANGE

Each partner in the overfunctioning-underfunctioning dance resists changing the steps they know so well. Overfunctioners have a strong will not to change, because in this dance they never have to see their faults. The fear of emotional pain keeps them stuck in patterns that are familiar but unproductive. They are less willing than an underfunctioner to look at their steps or missteps. Part of their healing process is to learn the disciplines of solitude in listening to the Holy Spirit and submission to God's way of working out the new dance.

Underfunctioners fear the overfunctioner's reaction to changing steps and shut themselves down to needed change. However, the underfunctioner must start looking at their steps that maintain the dance instead of always blaming the problem on the overfunctioner. It's important that they break down their denial and acknowledge all that they are getting from the overfunctioner's overstepping their steps. For the underfunctioner, anger, depression, and anxiety are SOS alerts that the dance is out of sync with their well-being.

Galatians 6:2 and 5 becomes the new theme song of change for relationships trying to break this pattern: "Bear one another's burdens, and thus fulfill the law of Christ...For each one shall bear his own load."

The all-important "I" moves to the forefront of the new dance as each partner seeks first and only the focus of changing their own moves rather than changing the moves of their partner.

LEARNING A NEW DANCE IN LIFE

The following suggestions will insure continued success in maintaining a new and healthier dance with loved ones. No longer are we father-wounded destined to live in the past, but God calls us to a future of hope and growth.

1. Sort out the yours, mine, and ours of responsibility. Separate your responsibility from theirs.
2. Learn to clarify and define yourself to yourself and to others you are in relationship with.

3. Identify and take responsibility for your role in stuck relationships.
4. Accept responsibility for changing the legacy you carry from past generations. Make it stop with you!
5. Learn to stand beside others in their pain, rather than making them "all better."
6. Stay responsibly connected in the relationship within the boundaries you need to set to feel safe.
7. Overfunctioners need to share vulnerabilities, underfunctioners need to share competencies.
8. Learn to use the language of responsibility.

BLESSING ON YOUR HEALING

Thank you for picking up your "stuff" and letting me take you on this healing journey from childhood pain to peace in maturity. It has been a pleasure and an honor to be your escort into experiencing a deeper presence with our heavenly ABBA.

CHAPTER FOURTEEN

Group Study Questions

1. In what ways do you externalize problems in your significant relationships? Is Jesus' admonition in Matthew 7:3-5 ever applicable to your style of interacting?

2. What is your primary mode of defensiveness?

3. What is your conflict style from the ones discussed?

4. What are your "trigger issues" or areas of woundedness that you get angry or defensive about?

5. What one area can you commit to using the "clarification process" with your significant other this week? What new, more responsible behaviors will you use in approaching your loved ones this week?

Appendix A: The Blessing

God's Thoughts Toward You

For I know the thoughts that I think toward you, saith the Lord, thoughts of peace, and not of evil, to give you an expected end.

—Jeremiah 29:11 KJV

It is My desire that you know My thoughts toward you that your eyes be opened and your mind enlightened that you may know and understand.

I want you to know the rich glory of your inheritance in ME, and My incomparably great power that is in you. I want your mind renewed by the same mighty power that raised Me from the dead and seated Me in the place of honor at God's right hand in heaven.

The Father holds you snugly in His thoughts with love. His thoughts and plans for you are good and hold glory beyond your dreams.

Release yourself from the prison of human reasoning. You have been a prisoner of lies. You have believed that you are not worthy of being gloriously blessed. Do not think you were called to live a life of heartache. You have considered yourself an outcast, one whom no one seeks after and for whom no one cares. Even if you have not spoken these thoughts aloud, you have allowed them to be your master. I will heal your wounds, and release you from these chains of despair into the arms of Love. Choose love and goodness from this day on. No longer accept a life under the oppressor's yoke.

You shall no more be a slave of ungodly lusts and passions and lack of self-respect.

My loving thoughts toward you also break the chains of pride. You need not defend yourself, clawing so frantically, like a cat thrown in water. I am the One who defends you. I am rich in mercy toward you. It is My will that you open the eyes of your heart and see what an incredible quality of love the Father has given you through Me.

Jeremiah 30:17
Ephesians 1:18-20
(Adapted from Chapian, Marie, *God's Thoughts Toward You*)

Appendix B: Feelings List

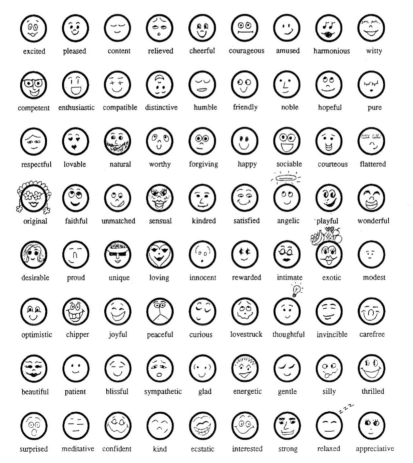

excited	pleased	content	relieved	cheerful	courageous	amused	harmonious	witty
competent	enthusiastic	compatible	distinctive	humble	friendly	noble	hopeful	pure
respectful	lovable	natural	worthy	forgiving	happy	sociable	courteous	flattered
original	faithful	unmatched	sensual	kindred	satisfied	angelic	playful	wonderful
desirable	proud	unique	loving	innocent	rewarded	intimate	exotic	modest
optimistic	chipper	joyful	peaceful	curious	lovestruck	thoughtful	invincible	carefree
beautiful	patient	blissful	sympathetic	glad	energetic	gentle	silly	thrilled
surprised	meditative	confident	kind	ecstatic	interested	strong	relaxed	appreciative

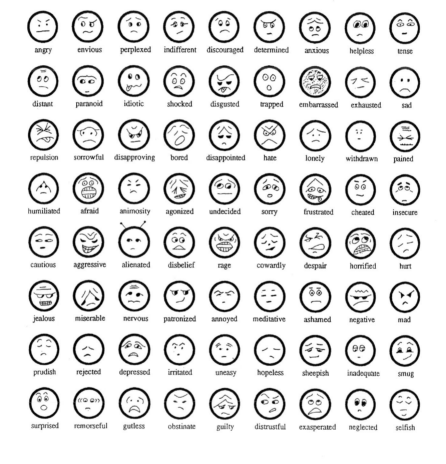

angry	envious	perplexed	indifferent	discouraged	determined	anxious	helpless	tense
distant	paranoid	idiotic	shocked	disgusted	trapped	embarrassed	exhausted	sad
repulsion	sorrowful	disapproving	bored	disappointed	hate	lonely	withdrawn	pained
humiliated	afraid	animosity	agonized	undecided	sorry	frustrated	cheated	insecure
cautious	aggressive	alienated	disbelief	rage	cowardly	despair	horrified	hurt
jealous	miserable	nervous	patronized	annoyed	meditative	ashamed	negative	mad
prudish	rejected	depressed	irritated	uneasy	hopeless	sheepish	inadequate	smug
surprised	remorseful	gutless	obstinate	guilty	distrustful	exasperated	neglected	selfish

Appendix C: Visualization Exercises for Chapters Eight and Twelve

CHAPTER EIGHT VISUALIZATION

Today you are going to take a final walk with the dad of your past. Get yourself into a comfortable position and close your eyes. As you begin to take deep relaxing breaths, I would like you to visualize your father standing in front of you. You can make him whichever memory seems best to you. For instance, he can be the dad of your grade school years or your adolescence, whichever seems right for you. You and your dad begin to walk down a country road. As you walk down this road, think about and color in the scenery around you. Are you basking in the heat of summer, a crisp and colorful autumn, the frosty crunch of winter, or the freshness of spring?

Pacing yourself to your father's stride you look at him out of the corner of your eye, noting every detail of this picture of him that you remember. As you walk along with him, the two of you come upon an old-fashioned railway station. You climb the steps and approach the ticket agent, purchasing one one-way ticket. In the distance, you hear the train's whistle as it approaches. The ticket agent says your train will be departing in about five minutes. As the train pulls into the station, you turn to this dad of your past for one last good-bye. You may want to hug him, pat his shoulder, or just wave good-bye.

Do whatever good-bye gesture that seems right for how you feel about this dad of your past.

When the conductor announces, "All aboard!" you mount the steps and take a seat by the window. As the train begins to pull out of the station, you lift your hand and wave as it moves slowly away from the platform. You keep looking back at your dad until he is but a speck on the horizon. As you turn around in your seat, you are quiet in your heart and your thoughts for awhile, knowing that this segment of your life with this father is over. Later, as you begin to come out of private thoughts, you begin to notice life around you inside the rail car and outside in the countryside. Life is moving on. You look up and face forward as you begin to contemplate your future, asking yourself, "Where is this train taking me? What does God have in store for me as this chapter closes and a new one opens?"

(After you use this visualization, take some time to record your feelings and emotions as you leave this dad behind and move on.)

CHAPTER TWELVE VISUALIZATION

Get in a relaxed position, close your eyes, and allow the Holy Spirit to use your imagination in your mind's eye to give you some direction. As you take long, slow, deep breaths, picture yourself in the safest place in your life. It doesn't matter whether it's inside, outside, at home, the past, present, childhood, etc., as long as it is a place that feels safe for you.

As you picture yourself standing in your safe place, I would like you to turn and face the east. The sun comes up in the east every morning and signals a new beginning in a new day. What new beginning is God showing you? After you have received this piece, turn a quarter turn and face the south in your safe place. We think of the south bringing warm breezes and a sense of comfort and security. What is God providing in the way of warmth and security in your life during this season? After He reveals this, then turn a quarter turn to the west. Here the sun sets every day signaling the end of another day and the time to rest. What is God asking you to let go of and release to Him? How will He rest you? Finally, take a quarter turn to the north. The winds of change blow out of the north. What changes are blowing into your life right now? What does God want to change in you?

As you're looking down pondering these new truths, you realize that there is something that holds you or draws you to earth. You ponder the miracle of gravity, realizing there are things that anchor you and keep you centered in life. What would those things be for you? Another place you seek direction is to look up when you pray, perhaps into the blue sky. As you consider new directions or endeavors God wants you to accomplish in the future, what would those directions be?

After a little while as you're contemplating these words from the Lord, a person whom you consider to be very wise in your life enters your safe place. This wise person begins to unfold to you truths about yourself that you have not known before. You listen to these pieces of wise truth, and then you notice a small child peeking at you from around the corner. You and your wise person look at each other and you beckon the child to come on in. This child comes over to you and wants to be held by you. Your wise person indicates that it would be OK for you to take this child into your arms. As you do so, your wise person tells you that this child is really you. In profound wonder, you watch as this child tries to connect with you. Finally, you cannot help but respond. Sooner, rather than later, the child gets restless and would like to leave and take you on a picnic.

You, your wise person, and this child depart to a grassy country meadow where you enjoy a picnic lunch. After lunch, the child wants to go play in a Disneyland-like park that is set up here in the meadow. And so for several hours, you, your wise person, and this child ride rides and play games to your heart's content.

Several hours later, the child tells you he/she is tired and needs to leave. However, before he/she goes, he hands you a gift. You open the gift in front of your wise person and find it to be something very special to the three of you. As you leave the meadow this day, you know that this is not the last time that you will visit this place. You, your child, and your wise person will return in the future to play and come together again.

Appendix D: The Crazymakers of Relationships

*A*n Avoider: These individuals refuse to stay and fight when conflict arises. They either fall sleep, run away, distract themselves with work, TV, sports, kids, or computers (to name a few) so they will not have to face a problem head on. For a partner living with an avoider, it's like trying to box with someone who won't show up for the match!

A **Guiltmaker:** The guiltmaker loves to play the martyr. They will never tell you directly when they disapprove. They will just say with a huge sigh, "That's OK, don't worry about me," which causes the other person to feel guilty and responsible for the guiltmaker's unhappiness.

A **Subject Changer:** Obviously these people practice avoidance by switching subjects when conflicts arise. This practice ends up frustrating partners, because nothing ever gets resolved as long as a subject changer is on the run!

A **Distracter:** A distracter doesn't talk about what's really bugging them. Instead, they will pick apart other aspects of their partner's life and habits.

A **Crisis Tickler:** A crisis tickler is similar to a distracter in that they don't bring up what's really bothering them directly. Instead of saying directly, "I'm afraid we're not going to have enough to pay the bills this month," they will ask, "Gee, how much did that cost?"

A **Mindreader:** A mindreader is more interested in character analysis, diagnosing, and labeling the other person's problems than in honestly listening to how the other person feels. In this way, they avoid their own feelings and problems and shut down their partner in expressing themselves.

A **Trapper:** Trappers will set you up by asking for a certain behavior, and then when you perform it, they will attack you for doing it or how you do it. Self-disclosure is never safe in the company of a trapper.

A **Gunnysacker:** This individual gets their name because they keep "bagging" all their frustration and resentment towards others in a huge gunnysack until it's bulging over with large and small gripes. Then they explode all over an unsuspecting victim.

A **Trivial Tyrannizer:** These people bring passive-aggression to a new level by doing little things to get even in relationships, instead of honestly sharing their feelings and resentments. They often focus exclusively on pet peeves of the other person, like clipping their toenails in bed and leaving them, belching out loud, keeping the television so loud that it drowns out any conversation, etc.

A **Beltliner:** Most individuals have an invisible boundary called a "beltline," and below it are sensitive subjects that the other person usually can't help, or they're traits the other person is trying to overcome. A beltliner will purposefully harp on these things in order to get even by hitting below the belt, so they're sure to return hurt for hurt to the other person.

A **Joker:** Jokers clown around about everything, even when their partner wants them to discuss a situation seriously. A type of avoidance, jokers have fun at the expense of cutting themselves and others off from facing their true feelings.

A **Contract Tyrannizer:** Having a relationship with a contract tyrannizer is having a relationship in stone. The relationship doesn't ever change in responsibility or role. Each person has their specific role or job forever. It's your job to cook, wash the dishes, discipline the kids, etc.

A **Kitchen Sink Fighter:** If you fight with this person, expect that you will hear about everything but the "kitchen sink," i.e. the way you pronouce your "Rs", what you did on New Year's Eve two years ago, your spending habits, etc.

A Blamer: A blamer is more interested in pointing the finger at you and making the issue solely your fault than really working on conflicts. This type of behavior usually triggers more defensiveness in relationships than truly working things out fairly.

A Withholder: These individuals are very passive-aggressive, choosing to express their frustration in relationships indirectly through holding back something like conversation, kindness, cooking, sex, humor, etc.

A Benedict Arnold: Undermining and sabotage characterize the indirect attacks of a Benedict Arnold. They prove themselves untrustworthy in relationships, because not only will they not support and defend their partners in conflicts, they will actually contribute and invite ridicule from others toward that person.

This list of Crazymakers was adapted and expanded from the basic concepts of George Bach and Peter Wyeden in *The Intimate Enemy* (1968) Avon Books, New York, NY and George Bach Aggression *Lab: The Fair Fight Manual* (1971) Kendall-Hunt, Dubuque, IA.

Endnotes

PREFACE

1. Ancona, Frank, *Crisis in America: Father Absence,* (1998) Nova Science Publishers, Commack, NY.
2. Lewis, Paul, *The 5 Key Habits of Smart Dads,* (1996) Zondervan Publishing, Grand Rapids, MI. p. 23-24.

CHAPTER ONE

1. *Baker Encyclopedia of Psychology,* (1985) David G. Benner, ed., Baker Book House, Grand Rapids, MI, p. 1173.
2. Meier, P. Minirth, F., Wichern, F., *Introduction to Psychology and Counseling* (1982) Baker Book House, Grand Rapids, MI, p. 346.
3. *Baker Encyclopedia of Psychology,* (1985) David G. Benner, ed., Baker Book House, Grand Rapids, MI, p. 79.
4. Drew, Jane M., *Where Were You When I Needed You Dad?* (1991) Tiger Lily Publishing, Newport Beach, CA.
5. Justice, W.G. & Lambert, W., (1986) A comparative study of the language people use to describe the personalities of God and their earthly parents. The *Journal of Pastoral Care* 40:166-72.
6. Dickie, J.R., Eschleman A.K., Merasco, D.M., Shepard, A., Vanderwilt, M., Johnson, M., (1997) "Parent Child Relationships

and Children's Images of God." *Journal for the Scientific Study of Religion,* 36(1):25-43.

CHAPTER TWO

1. Erickson, Beth M., (1996) "Men's Unresolved Father Hunger: Intervention and Primary Prevention," *Journal of Family Psychotherapy,* 7(4): 37-62.
2. Piaget, J., (1932) *The Moral Judgment of the Child.* Glencoe, IL: Free Press, 1948 (first edition, 1932).
3. Ibid.
4. Cloud, H. & Townsend, J., (1992) *Boundaries,* Zondervan, Grand Rapids, MI.
5. Erickson, Beth M., (1996) "Men's Unresolved Father Hunger: Intervention and Primary Prevention," *Journal of Family Psychotherapy,* 7(4): 37-62.
6. Festinger, L., (1957) A theory of cognitive dissonance. Stanford, CA: Stanford University.
7. Chapian, Marie, *His Thoughts Toward Me,* (1987) Bethany House Publishers, Minneapolis, MN.
8. Brunner, R.A. (1993) Personality and demographic correlates of the God-concept. Dissertation Abstracts International. Vol. 53 (12-A), Jun 1993, 4205.
9. Dickie, J.R., Eshleman, A.K., Merasco, D.M., Shepard, A., Vanderwilt, M., Johnson, M., (1997) "Parent-child Relationships and Children's Images of God," *Journal for the Scientific Study of Religion,* vol. 36(1), Mar 1997, 25-43.

CHAPTER THREE

1. Cloud, H. & Townsend, J. (1992) *Boundaries,* Zondervan Publishing House, Grand Rapids, MI, p.33.
2. Ibid., p. 31.
3. Kushner, Harold S. (1981) *When Bad Things Happen to Good People,* AVON Books, New York, NY, p. 43.
4. Yancey, Philip (1988) *Disappointment with God,* HarperCollins Publishers, New York, NY, p. 213.
5. Ibid., p. 247.
6. Ibid.

7. Ibid., p. 248.

CHAPTER FOUR

1. Adler, R.B. & Towne, N. (1999) *Looking Out Looking In,* Harcourt Brace & Company, 6277 Sea Harbor Drive, Orlando, FL, p.51-52.
2. Ibid., p.59.
3. Van Vonderen, J. (1989) *Tired of Trying to Measure Up,* Bethany House Publishers, Minneapolis, MN, p.19.
4. Ibid., p. 23.
5. Elwell, W.A., ed. (1984) *Evangelical Dictionary of Theology,* Baker Book House, Grand Rapids, MI, p. 545.
6. Barker, K., ed. (1995) *The NIV Study Bible,* Zondervan Publishing, Grand Rapids, MI, study notes, p. 8.
7. Day, L. G. (1992) *By Design and in God's Image,* Mt. Tabor Press, Portland, OR, p.56-57.
8. Adler, R.B. & Towne, N. (1999) *Looking Out Looking In,* Harcourt Brace & Company, 6277 Sea Harbor Drive, Orlando, FL p. 53.

CHAPTER FIVE

1. Day, Larry G. (1975) "The Development of the God Concept: A Symbolic Interaction Approach," *Journal of Psychology and Theology,* Rosemead Graduate School of Professional Psychology, La Mirada, CA, Vol.3:3, p. 172-178.
2. Erickson, Beth (1998) "Long for Dad: Father Loss and Its Impact," Health Communications, Deerfield Beach, FL, p. 86.
3. Dalbey, Gordon (1988) *Healing the Masculine Soul,* WORD Publishing, Dallas, TX, p.43.
4. Molotsky, Irvin, *New York Times* News Service "Study Links Absentee Fathers, Troubled Kids," reprinted in *The Oregonian,* Aug. 31, 1999, Portland, Oregon.
5. Wolgemuth, Robert (1999) *She Calls Me Daddy,* Tyndale House Publishers, Wheaton, IL, p. 59.
6. Lewis, Paul (1994) *The Five Key Habits of Smart Dads,* Zondervan Publishing House, Grand Rapids, MI, p.46.
7. Ibid., p. 48.

8. Payne, Leanne (1986) *Crisis in Masculinity,* Crossway Books, Westchester, IL, p.46.
9. Lewis, Paul (1994) *The Five Key Habits of Smart Dads,* Zondervan Publishing House, Grand Rapids, MI, p. 46.
10. Roberts, Ted (1999) *Pure Desire,* Regal Books, Ventura, CA, p.65

CHAPTER SIX

1. Ghezzi, B. &Kinzer, M. (1983) *Emotions As Resources,* Servant Books, Ann Arbor, MI, p. 19.
2. Adler, R.B. & Towne, N. (1999) *Looking Out Looking In,* Harcourt Brace & Company, 6277 Sea Harbor Drive, Orlando, FL p. 159.
3. Ghezzi, B. & Kinzer, M. (1983) *Emotions As Resources,* Servant Books, Ann Arbor, MI, p. 18.
4. Adler, R.B. & Towne, N. (1999) *Looking Out Looking In,* Harcourt Brace & Company, 6277 Sea Harbor Drive, Orlando, FL, p. 160.

CHAPTER SEVEN

1. Adler, R.B. & Towne, N. (1999) *Looking Out Looking In,* Harcourt Brace & Company, 6277 Sea Harbor Drive, Orlando, FL p. 100.

CHAPTER EIGHT

1. Yancey, Philip (1999) *What's So Amazing about Grace,* Zondervan, Grand Rapids, MI, p. 127.
2. Ibid., p. 127.
3. Ibid., p. 129.
4. Ibid., p. 137.

CHAPTER NINE

1. Missildine, W. H. (1963) *Your Inner Child of the Past,* Simon and Schuster Inc., New York, NY, p.4.

2. Adler, R.B. & Towne, N. (1999) *Looking Out, Looking In,* 9th edition, Harcourt Brace College Publications, Fort Worth, TX, p. 8-9.
3. Ells, A. H. (1992) *One-Way Relationships-Workbook,* Thomas Nelson Publishers, Nashville, TN, p. 53.

CHAPTER TEN

1. Drew, Jane M. (1991) *Where Were You When I Needed You Dad?,* Tiger Lily Publishing,

CHAPTER ELEVEN

1. Chapian, Marie (1987) *His Thoughts Toward Me,* Bethany House Publishers, Minneapolis, MN.
2. Strunk, O. (1959) "Perceived Relationships Between Parental and Deity Concepts," *Psychological Newsletter,* 12:222-26.
3. Yancey, Philip (1999) *What's So Amazing About Grace?* Harper Collins Publishers, New York, NY.
4. Drew, Jane M. (1991) *Where Were You When I Needed You Dad?,* Tiger Lily Publishing.

CHAPTER THIRTEEN

1. Adapted and expanded from M. L. Knapp and A.L. Vangelisti, *Interpersonal Communication and Human Relationships,* 2d ed., Allyn and Bacon, Boston, MA, pp. 32-56.
2. Adler, R.B. & Towne, N. (1999) *Looking Out, Looking In,* 9th edition, Harcourt Brace College Publications, Fort Worth, TX, p. 338-339.
3. Drew, Jane M. (1991) *Where Were You When I Needed You Dad?,* Tiger Lily Publishing, p.169.
4. Ibid., p. 169.
5. Adler, R.B. & Towne, N. (1999) *Looking Out, Looking In,* 9th edition, Harcourt Brace College Publications, Fort Worth, TX, p.400-405, 413-423.

CHAPTER FOURTEEN

1. Drew, Jane M. (1991) *Where Were You When I Needed You Dad?*, Tiger Lily Publishing.
2. Roberts, Ted, Senior Pastor, East Hill Church, Gresham, OR.
3. Drew, Jane M., (1991) *Where Were You When I Needed You Dad?*, Tiger Lily Publishing.

LaVergne, TN USA
26 April 2010
180569LV00002B/16/P